CUSTOMER SERVICE MANAGEMENT TRAINING 101

QUICK AND EASY TECHNIQUES THAT GET GREAT RESULTS

Renée Evenson

AMACOM

New York • Atlanta • Brussels • Chicago • Mexico City
San Francisco • Shanghai • Tokyo • Washington, D. C

Bulk discounts available. For details visit:
www.amacombooks.org/go/specialsales
Or contact special sales:
Phone: 800-250-5308
E-mail: specialsls@amanet.org
View all the AMACOM titles at: www.amacombooks.org

This publication is designed to provide accurate and authoritative information in regard to the subject matter covered. It is sold with the understanding that the publisher is not engaged in rendering legal, accounting, or other professional service. If legal advice or other expert assistance is required, the services of a competent professional person should be sought.

Library of Congress Cataloging-in-Publication Data

Evenson, Renee, 1951–
    Customer service management training 101 : quick and easy techniques that get great results / Renee Evenson. — 1st ed.
        p.   cm.
    Includes index.
    ISBN-13: 978-0-8144-1715-7
    ISBN-10: 0-8144-1715-9
    1. Customer services—Management. 2. Executives—Training of. 3. Time management. 4. Leadership. 5. Communication in management. I. Title.
    HF5415.5E894   2011
    658.3′1245—dc23

                                                                        2011019828

About AMA
American Management Association (www.amanet.org) is a world leader in talent development, advancing the skills of individuals to drive business success. Our mission is to support the goals of individuals and organizations through a complete range of products and services, including classroom and virtual seminars, webcasts, webinars, podcasts, conferences, corporate and government solutions, business books, and research. AMA's approach to improving performance combines experiential learning—learning through doing—with opportunities for ongoing professional growth at every step of one's career journey.

Printing number
10 9 8 7 6 5 4 3 2 1

This book is dedicated to my husband, Joe, for his help and support,

*To my beautiful family, friends, and menagerie of pets who
each, in some way, teach me how to be my best,*

*And to my parents who, by their examples,
taught me the importance of living well.*

CONTENTS

ACKNOWLEDGMENTS

My sincere and heartfelt thanks to each of you for helping me as I wrote this book:

My editor, Bob Nirkind. You truly are the best editor any author could hope for. Your involvement and continued support throughout the writing process helped me be a better writer and kept me on track.

My agent, Michael Snell, for believing in my talent and strength as a writer.

My copyeditor, Barbara Chernow and Associates, for your amazing attention to detail. I learn so much from you with each book I write.

My proofreaders, Rose and Joe, who give me honest feedback, even when I don't want to hear it—you are good at targeting the small stuff.

My clients for being my best supporters, as well as critics.

My deepest appreciation for each of you for all you to do make me a better person.

Introduction

Why do customers take their business elsewhere? Some move away. Some are not satisfied with the product. Some go for competitive reasons. But the majority of customers take their business elsewhere because the business owner, manager, or frontline employee is indifferent toward them. Most of these customers will not even complain; they just won't come back.

Great customer service isn't doing *what you think* your customers want; it's doing *what* your customers want. One of the biggest mistakes businesses make is assuming they know what their customers want without getting to know their customers and their needs. Managers who ensure that they and their teams are clued in to their customers are in the best position to give exceptional service.

To understand customers, you need to get close to them, stay tuned in to them, and think like them. Frontline employees are the key. They present the face of the business, so it is crucial that managers train them to interact successfully with customers. Customer service managers who know how to train effectively, follow up with observation, and provide meaningful feedback are in a great position to develop customer loyalty.

Every customer service manager wants to develop strong teams in which coworkers interact well with each other and take responsibility for providing exceptional customer service. But although they understand how important customer service is, many acknowledge that their employees often do not appreciate its importance. In addition, managers often ignore employee behavior problems because they do not know how to deal with them. The sad news, for managers, is that ignoring problems will not make them go away. Ignoring problems *will* make customers go away.

Managers interested in learning how to motivate employees to provide top-notch service will find their answers by reading *Customer Service Management Training 101*. This book teaches managers how to be effective leaders and how to develop the necessary skills to communicate, train, and inspire their frontline employees who are responsible for customer satisfaction. It is also a good teaching tool for personal skills development.

Customer Service Management Training 101 utilizes the successful format of *Customer Service Training 101*, providing step-by-step lessons to help new managers become effective leaders and veteran managers improve their skills. It is divided into three parts: managing yourself, managing others, and managing for results.

Each chapter includes a skills checklist, a "real world" practice lesson, and a goal planner. Chapter topics include understanding your personal management style; developing solid leadership qualities; planning and organizing; communicating up, down, across, inside, and outside; training for excellence; building a strong team; monitoring performance; providing meaningful feedback; and finally, focusing on self-development and making yourself the best you can be.

Customer Service Management Training 101 will endure because it focuses on managing and leading frontline employees to provide exceptional customer service. While other aspects of a business undergo continual change, the fundamentals of customer service management remain the same.

The most important benefit of being an effective customer service manager is increased productivity, efficiency, and job satisfaction. It is always cheaper and faster when frontline employees do the job right the first time. Satisfying an unhappy customer costs a lot more, both in dollars and time, than satisfying a customer on the first try.

As a manager, your success depends not only on how well you perform, but on how well your employees perform. Your success depends on your mastery of leadership and management skills. Whether you are a new manager or a veteran, *Customer Service Management Training 101* will help you get to the top of your game—and stay there.

PART ONE

MANAGING YOURSELF

1

Understanding Your Management Style

Frontline management is not easy. You have employees for whom you are responsible. You have a manager to whom you report. And you are, quite frankly, caught in the middle. The expectation of your employees to get results while responding to your own manager's needs can leave you feeling overwhelmed. How do you do it all without cracking under the stress?

In addition to having employee and upper management responsibilities, you are also accountable for customer satisfaction, for ensuring that your employees provide exceptional customer service to every customer all the time. How do you accomplish that goal, especially when you are keeping so many balls in the air?

Well-trained frontline employees are your key to customer satisfaction, and knowledgeable and engaged managers are the key to well-trained employees. By effectively training, observing, and motivating, your employees will learn to do their best and that will result in the level of customer service that both your company and customers expect.

Customer Service Is Job #1

Customer service may not be your only job duty, but it is the most important one. As a frontline manager, your success depends not only on how well you perform, but on how well your employees perform. In other words, your success depends on your mastery of leadership and management skills and how well you are able to transfer those skills to your employees.

The first step to becoming a successful manager is to understand and identify your personal management style. Knowing who you are, how you communicate, and why you behave as you do helps you develop the positive skills that result in effective management.

The truth is that not every manager is a good manager. Some lead by controlling others, taking an upper-handed authoritative approach, with little or no trust in their employees. Others lead passively, taking a hands-off approach and wanting more to be liked by their employees than to manage them. The most successful managers take a hands-on, participative approach and find the balance between being controlling and remaining passive depending on the employee and the circumstances.

By learning about different management styles and characteristics, you can assess your personal style and determine your strengths, as well as identify areas needing improvement. When you define those strengths and, more importantly, see where improvement is needed, you can create a developmental action plan and move toward becoming the manager your employees and coworkers appreciate and value.

Remember that your success is directly linked to how well your employees perform. While it is great to be liked by your employees, it is more important to have their respect. When you follow the steps below, you will develop effective management skills that will earn the respect of both your employees and coworkers.

STEP 1: Learn Management Styles and Functions

STEP 2: Analyze Your Personal Style

STEP 3: Define Your Strengths and Areas Needing Improvement

STEP 4: Create Your Developmental Action Plan

SPOTLIGHT ON MANAGEMENT

The Wrong Way to Manage the Frontline

Jack, a frontline manager for a large office supply chain, manages ten sales employees. He is a gregarious man who likes to tell jokes and make others laugh. To be well-liked means a lot to him. He read somewhere that it is important to have fun on the job, so he manages by making sure his employees are having a good time.

Jack does a great job training new employees, but he does little follow-up to make sure they are doing their jobs correctly. He also allows his employees to hang out in his office and does not feel comfortable telling them to get back to work. Consequently, customers are often left to wander around the store when employees are in his office joking and having fun.

One day, before storming out of the store, an irate customer said to one of the employees, "I've been walking around this store for ten minutes, and no one has come to help me. I just wanted to let you know I'm going to the store down the street where I know they appreciate my business."

Later, when the employee was in Jack's office relating this conversation, another employee asked, "What high horse did he ride in on?" Everyone laughed, but Jack knew he should have done something to prevent the situation from occurring in the first place.

What Went Wrong?

Jack tends to be a passive manager. Because he wants his employees to like him, he did not take the necessary measures to ensure they were putting customers first. He hoped his employees knew what to do, but when they did not demonstrate that knowledge, Jack did not speak up and change the situation. Rather than being more assertive when he needed to, he sat back. When the employee made a disparaging comment about the customer, Jack laughed along with the employees rather than pointing out their mistake.

What Could Make This Right?

Jack never took the time to assess his management style, define his strengths and areas needing improvement, or create a developmental action plan. Honest self-analysis and skills development could have helped him find the balance he needed to manage effectively—and still create a happy work environment.

STEP 1: Learn Management Styles and Functions

The most important function of frontline management is to lead and develop employees. When you manage people your job is to accomplish tasks and achieve goals through your employees. How you achieve this result depends on the employees and the circumstances.

The methods you most often apply to employee interactions and various situations define your personal management style. Your management style determines how you communicate, make decisions, solve problems, and put your critical thinking skills to use. The most effective managers do not apply the same style all the time. Rather, they are able to adapt their style as needed.

The study of management has been widely researched. Similar managerial styles, ranging from overly controlling to a complete lack of control, emerge. The style now viewed as the most effective is participative. Yet, researchers also conclude that participative management actually incorporates both controlling and passive behavior, depending on the environment.

In this chapter, three distinct styles of management will be discussed. They are shown on the continuum below. A continuum is a plotting tool that uses a continuous line with varying points of reference placed along it. Later in this chapter, you will plot your personal management style. Most likely, after analyzing your behavior, you are going to find that your comfort zone falls somewhere to the left or right of participative, depending on your personality and experience level.

Controlling   Participative   Passive

Controlling Management Is Autocratic Management

The controlling manager makes decisions for the team with no input or consultation with employees, preferring to tell them what to do. Communication is generally one-way from top to bottom, and the manager does more talking than listening.

This management style is effective when snap decisions must be made, when immediate action is necessary, when time constraints do not allow for employee input, when employee input is not warranted, or when employees are new to the task and have not been fully trained. It is least effective when used excessively or inappropriately. Employees lose motivation when they are not involved in decision making, and autocratic overuse can even lead to a hostile work environment in which employees feel they have no autonomy or are not empowered to do their jobs.

Autocratic management is no longer a desired approach to managing and most managers have abandoned it; those who still heavily rely on this approach are often labeled "dinosaurs."

Participative Management Is Shared Management

The participative manager applies a hands-on, involved approach, and both the manager and employees share in making decisions and solving problems. This manager knows his or her employees well, understands their strengths and weaknesses, and knows who functions best under this approach. Employee input is welcome and delegation of work is utilized. Communication is two-way and open.

This management style is effective when the manager takes the time to adequately train, observe, develop, and provide feedback to employees. When these steps are taken, employees feel engaged and empowered to perform at their best. This style is least effective when employee input is continually welcomed but not acted upon, when too much or not enough responsibility is shared with employees, or when work is delegated to employees who do not have the ability to complete the task.

Participative management emerged when team involvement, quality work groups, and self-managed teams became popular. Employee empowerment through the participative approach is now the widely accepted and preferred management style.

Passive Management Is Permissive Management

The passive manager takes a back seat and allows the team to make decisions, set goals, and achieve objectives. Communication is two-way, often adopting a democratic approach in which employees are given equal power with the manager for making decisions.

This management style is effective when employees have been well trained, are high achievers who work as a cohesive unit, and have displayed sound decision-making and problem solving techniques. It is last effective when teams have not reached the cohesive stage of development or when the manager uses it to avoid making decisions or resolving conflict. Overuse of this approach can lead to a lack of focus and direction, or even more serious, a lack of respect by the employees.

Passive management, while not the ideal style of managing when utilized excessively, can be appropriate when employees have proved they deserve empowerment and control. Teams can self-manage, with the manager remaining involved.

Management Functions Dictate the Management Style

As a manager, you are responsible for many tasks, which can be linked to three general functions: managing yourself, managing others, and managing results.

Managing yourself involves understanding your management style, as well as your strengths and weaknesses. It includes personal skills development, mapping out a plan to meet company objectives for both yourself and your team, defining how and when you will complete tasks and meet company commitments, and managing your time effectively.

Managing others involves encouraging them to share your vision and goals. It includes communicating effectively, training employees to do the job correctly, building a cohesive team, and effectively resolving conflicts and problems.

Managing results involves measuring and controlling outcomes. It includes analyzing goal achievement, observing, providing feedback, appraising, creating development action plans for employees, and monitoring self-development goals.

Each of these functions involves the ability to use your critical thinking skills to make decisions and solve problems. You must decide whether to control the events, allow employees to participate in them, or give employees complete freedom over them. An effective and successful manager knows which style to use for each function and when to change an approach as needed.

STEP 2: Analyze Your Management Style

You have learned about three management styles. You have also learned that the most effective approach is the participative style, which means having the ability to move left or right on the continuum, depending on the environment. Although the ability to move back and forth easily across the continuum will increase your effectiveness, you are probably more comfortable to the right or left of participative management. When push comes to shove, when time does not permit for participation, or when you are stressed out and overworked, you may not move easily across the continuum, but rather get stuck on one spot. You feel more comfortable either controlling the events or sitting back and hoping your employees do the right thing.

Analyzing how you perform on a daily basis will help you pinpoint the spot on the continuum that is your comfort zone. That spot defines your current personal style. Once you establish your comfort zone, you will then be able to assess areas that need improvement in order to develop the skills to move easily among all three styles as appropriate and necessary.

Honest Analysis Enables You to Define Your Management Style

Unless your self-assessment is honest, you will never be able to advance your development. Draw the continuum on a piece of paper. Write *Controlling* on the left, *Participative* in the middle, and *Passive* on the right. Think of your performance at work and then honestly assess where you fall on the continuum.

Begin by asking yourself the following questions:

✓ What decision-making techniques do I employ?

✓ How do I handle conflict and problems?

✓ How do I manage when I am under undue stress?

✓ How well do I know my employees' strengths and weaknesses?

✓ How effectively do I delegate?

✓ Do I find it difficult to control when I need to? Or, am I overly controlling when a more passive approach would be better?

How you manage depends on a number of variables. An experienced manager may feel more comfortable relying on a controlling approach.

If you are a new manager dealing with an experienced employee, you may take a passive approach, whereas with a new employee, you may feel more comfortable controlling the situation when necessary. If you have developed your skills sufficiently, you can effectively move among controlling, participative, or passive, depending on the circumstances. No matter your experience level, no matter the experience level of your employees, no answer is right or wrong. At this time, you are merely determining your comfort zone. Pinpointing where you fall on the continuum will assist you when you define your strengths and areas needing improvement.

You Are Most Comfortable Taking a Controlling Approach

You find it easier to tell people what to do rather than ask for their opinions. You are a good decision maker, so why bother wasting your employees' time asking for input that you most likely will not act on?

You feel comfortable setting goals for your team. You take full responsibility for employee training and development. When conflict occurs, you handle the situation by making the call and letting the involved parties know what you decided.

You understand the importance of developing your employees by delegating work, but depending on the task and time, you may prefer doing it yourself because you know it will be quicker than taking the time to explain the task to others.

You value the importance of being a participative manager, but efficiency is most important to you. Thus, when you are short on time, telling is the most efficient means of getting the job done.

You Are Most Comfortable Taking a Participative Approach

You are a people person who appreciates the opportunity to encourage a supportive, open atmosphere. You know your employees and have defined their strengths and weaknesses. You like to discuss problems, decisions, and outcomes with your team but you also feel comfortable either making the final decision or allowing your team the freedom to make the call, as appropriate. If you make the final decision, you take the time to explain your reasoning.

Goal setting is done by meeting with your employees and encouraging them to provide input and reach consensus. You make sure your employees are well-trained and, when possible, you rely on experienced team members to conduct the training. You value the importance of employee development and, when delegating work assignments, you take the time to ensure you are delegating to the person best suited for the task.

Rather than telling people what to do, you engage them in discussions and encourage them to take responsibility. When conflict arises, you work with the involved parties to find a win-win solution. Employee involvement, empowerment, and open communication are important to you.

You Are Most Comfortable Taking a Passive Approach

You do not feel comfortable telling people what to do. You would rather be viewed as one of the gang, rather than the boss. When a new employee joins your team, you trust your employees to help bring the new employee up to speed.

When discussing goals, you often agree with employees who complain how difficult it will be to attain them. You know you should delegate more because that will help your employees develop their skills, yet you find it challenging to because you are uncomfortable asking employees to take on additional responsibilities. You will do a task yourself rather than bothering an already overworked employee.

You do not like conflict and will often ignore it. When an employee brings a problem to you, you avoid dealing with it and hope the problem will resolve itself without your input. You just want a peaceful environment where everyone gets along.

Pinpoint Your Comfort Zone

After analyzing your personal style, let's assume you consider yourself a participative manager. You strive to manage your team by frequently discussing situations, involving them in decision making, and jointly setting goals. You see yourself as strong in valuing, supporting, and empowering your team. You know your employees and feel you make the correct moves across the continuum at all times. You are ready to plot your point on the continuum as participative.

But wait . . . let's say that after honestly analyzing your performance, you admit that you will often complete an assignment rather than delegate it because you prefer to avoid conflict of any kind. If your employees complain, you will often agree with them even when you know they are wrong. Bingo! Now you can pinpoint your style to the right of center on the continuum as participative/passive.

You should now see strengths and weaknesses emerging and begin to define each of them. Breaking out of your comfort zone is not going to be easy, but it is going to be worth it. Moving back and forth along the continuum easily and smoothly is an important goal for which to strive.

STEP 3: Define Your Strengths and Areas Needing Improvement

This is where the rubber meets the road. Now that you have assessed your personal management style, you need to define your specific strengths and weaknesses. Objectivity is important. Unless you can look at yourself objectively, you will never grow.

Start with Two Pieces of Paper with the Headings: (1) Management Skills and (2) Strengths and Areas Needing Improvement

When you write down relevant management skills, you have a good definition of all your work responsibilities. Similarly, when you write down your areas needing improvement and set concrete goals, you have a better chance of achieving them.

You will most likely be surprised when you list all the skills you need to do your job effectively. When it comes to strengths and areas needing improvement, you should have a good idea into which column each skill falls.

The only sure way to change a behavior is to acknowledge it, set a goal, and work toward achieving it. You know yourself better than anyone. Be honest when you write down areas requiring improvement. Then work on turning them into strengths.

Under "Skills," List Those That Are Important in Your Job

If this seems too daunting a task, think about what you do every day. What skills do you possess or need to possess to do your job effectively? To help you define which are important to your job, look through the contents of this book. Each chapter relates to one of the management functions you learned about in STEP 1: managing yourself, managing others, and managing results.

Conduct an Objective Analysis of Your Skills

For example, look at Chapter 4, "Communicating Up, Down, Across, In, and Out." Communication is a broad category, so review each item in that chapter and consider the ways in which you use those skills at work. Think also about feedback you receive on your communication skills.

Look at Step 1:"Listen Well."If you know that you make eye contact, listen actively and completely, and shut out distractions, then listening is probably one of your strengths. What about Step 3:"Speak Well"? Ask yourself whether, when you speak, the messages you send are received correctly. If you recall that you frequently have to rephrase or repeat, particularly with your employees, then that could be an area needing improvement. Think about each step in this chapter related to communicating up, down, across, within and outside your company. Think about what you do well and what you do not do well. Be completely objective and honest with yourself.

Under "Strengths and Areas Needing Improvement" Decide Where You Fall for Each Skill

Now that you have noted the skills required to do your job effectively, list each under the appropriate column. Conducting this analysis is going to take time, but assessing your abilities is crucial to your growth and development as a manager. Because you now understand your current management style, analyzing your strengths and areas needing improvement should be easier. Again, honesty is always the best policy. Being honest is a huge step to improving your skills.

STEP 4: Create Your Developmental Action Plan and Set Goals

Now that you completed your list, what do you do with it? Since your strengths are your assets, focus on those areas needing improvement. Creating your developmental action plan and setting goals is the next step in skills development.

Have Someone You Trust Review Your List

Before writing your development plan, ask someone you trust to sit down with you and go over your areas needing improvement. This could be a mentor, a coworker, or a friend. It is important that you ask someone who will remain unbiased and objective. Ask the person to read through both columns and give you feedback as to whether you should have listed a skill in the opposite column, or if there are any skills that you inadvertently omitted.

Meet With Your Boss for Feedback on Your List

Next, meet with your boss. Tell him or her that you are going to write a personal developmental action plan. However, before you prepare the plan, you would appreciate feedback on your strengths and areas needing improvement. Because you already had someone review the list with you, you should feel confident that you noted all pertinent skills in the correct columns. After agreeing on the list with your boss, state that after creating your development action plan you would like to meet again to review it.

Write Your Developmental Action Plan and Set Goals

Your action plan is your goal sheet. For each area of improvement, note the skill, what you need to do to develop this skill, and the date by which you will complete the necessary tasks. For example, if you listed making presentations to large groups as one of your areas needing improvement, consider the following. Is there in-house training available, or can you enroll in a class at your local college? What community groups can you join to develop this skill? What job tasks or projects can you take on in which you will need to make presentations? List all opportunities available that will help you. Note completion dates by each.

Meet Again with Your Boss to Finalize Your Plan

After creating your action plan/goal sheet, meet with your boss to review each item. If you were unable to come up with specific goals for an item, ask your boss to help you. Perhaps he or she can make a suggestion or offer to train or work with you.

Periodically Review Your Action Plan

Set a time schedule to go over your action plan. Every quarter will be a good starting point, particularly if you listed quite a few skills to work on. Think how great it will feel when you start moving areas needing improvement into your strength's column. When you conduct your analysis and can honestly assess that you move freely across the continuum depending on the employees and circumstances, you will have become a participative manager.

Remember, though, that we all have areas needing improvement. We are all a work in progress. Even if you can easily move along the continuum, you can still find a skill to develop or strengthen. Periodic self-analysis and continual self-awareness will only increase your effectiveness and keep you from falling back into old habits and behaviors.

SPOTLIGHT ON MANAGEMENT

A Better Way to Manage the Frontline

Jack had a wake-up call after the incident with the irate customer who stormed out of the store. He knew he messed up by being too lax with his employees. He knew they walked all over him, and he realized it was time to do something about that.

After reviewing STEP 1, he admitted that he fell into the participative/passive category. That was his comfort zone, and he did not stray too far from this spot on the continuum. He also admitted that by overusing this style, he was not an effective manager.

Next, he sat down to define his strengths and areas needing improvement. This was not difficult for Jack. He knew himself well; he just had never admitted how much his passivity hurt, not only himself and everyone on his team, but also relations with customers.

Two of the skills he listed under areas needing improvement were observing his employees and giving corrective feedback. He needed to be more hands-on, observe his employees' behaviors, and talk with them about correcting poor performance rather than sitting back and hoping they did the right thing.

After meeting with his general manager to review his developmental action plan, Jack read some management books that helped him improve his skills in these areas. He also asked his manager for help.

Then he held a meeting with his employees and explained that the day the customer stormed out of the store he understood that it was his responsibility to ensure it never happened again. "After all," he explained, "Without customers none of us would have jobs."

His next step was to hold customer care training sessions where he explained both corporate and his personal expectations for customer service. At first, his team was resistant. They also had developed their comfort zone of joking around rather than assisting customers.

"Look, I understand that things are going to be different. But they need to be. I take full responsibility for the relaxed atmosphere I created. That doesn't mean we can't still have fun. But it does mean that our customers are always going to come first, and we are going to do everything we can to help them." By assuring the team that Jack was still Jack, although a new and improved version, they bought into his expectations.

One day, when Jack observed an employee using a curt tone with a customer who had spoken rudely to her, he took her aside to talk about the situation. She complained, "That guy was such a jerk. I helped him but I was glad when he rode his high horse out of here."

This time Jack spoke up. "Look, let's not judge him or any of our customers. We don't know anyone's personal situations to comment about why they act as they do. Let's just do our best to help each customer who walks into our store. Remember, if customers stop coming, we're not needed."

CHECKLIST

STEP 1: Learn Management Styles and Functions

✓ Controlling management is autocratic management

✓ Participative management is shared management

✓ Passive management is permissive management

✓ Management functions dictate the management style

STEP 2: Analyze Your Management Style

✓ Honest analysis enables you to define your personal style

✓ You are most comfortable taking a controlling approach

✓ You are most comfortable taking a participatory approach

✓ You are most comfortable taking a passive approach

✓ Pinpoint your comfort zone

STEP 3: Define Your Strengths and Areas Needing Improvement

✓ Start with two pieces of paper with the headings (1) Management Skills and (2) Strengths and Areas Needing Improvement

✓ Under "Skills," list those that are important in doing your job

✓ Conduct an objective analysis of your skills

✓ Under "Strengths and Areas Needing Improvement," decide where you fall for each skill

STEP 4: Create Your Developmental Action Plan and Set Goals

✓ Have someone you trust review your list

✓ Meet with your boss for feedback on your list

✓ Write your developmental action plan and set goals

✓ Meet again with your boss to finalize your plan

✓ Periodically review your action plan

THE REAL WORLD

Practice Lesson

Ruth is a frontline manager in a call center. She prides herself on being a hands-on, involved manager who feels that employee development is her most important job. Before delegating work, she usually analyzes the situation carefully. But, when she is under pressure or gets backed up with her own work, she stresses out, becomes curt with her team members, and tells them what to do without their input.

Today, one of Ruth's employees walked into her office to ask a question about an assignment she had delegated to him. Ruth responded, "I already took the time to train you how to handle it. Right now I am too busy to train you again. Look, if you don't know what to do, just leave it here and I'll do it myself." She sighed loudly and looked down at the work on her desk. The employee, looking bewildered, left the work on her desk and walked out of her office.

Where does Ruth's management style fall on the continuum?

_____

_____

_____

Based on this scenario, list Ruth's strengths and areas needing improvement.

_____

_____

_____

Write out a developmental action plan for Ruth. Note her areas needing improvement, set goals, and, note time frames for completion dates (example: 1 month).

_____

_____

_____

PERSONAL PLANNER

Thoughts, ideas, and goals on your personal management style and development:

_____

_____

_____

_____

_____

_____

_____

_____

_____

_____

_____

_____

_____

_____

_____

_____

_____

_____

_____

_____

_____

_____

_____

_____

2

Developing Your Leadership Qualities

In Chapter 1, you learned about the three different management styles: controlling, participative, and passive. You may think that these management styles and leadership are really one and the same, but they are not. Managing is the process by which you direct and control outcomes. Leadership is the process through which you influence others to achieve your goals. In other words, it is how well you get your employees to achieve the outcomes you need.

When you take a controlling approach, you are directing rather than leading. When you take a passive approach, you are allowing others to take the lead. Only participative management and leadership go hand in hand. When you apply a participative management approach, your employees will want to follow your lead.

As a manager, you already know that to get results your employees must be behind you. They are the ones who get the job done for you. By developing your leadership qualities, you will learn how to get your employees behind you. That makes getting the job done much easier. But is it even possible to develop leadership qualities?

Leaders Take Responsibility to Give Great Service

The bottom line is yes. You can develop the qualities to lead effectively. As a frontline manager, you lead by example. When you put customers first, your employees will put customers first. When goal achievement is important to you, it will be important to your employees. When you are motivated, your employees will be motivated. When you work productively, your employees will work productively. By leading in a positive, participative manner, your employees will meet corporate and team goals, and they will give great service to each customer.

You may think that leaders are born with certain qualities that make them outstanding and different from the rest of us. While this is true for some people, most are not born with all the qualities necessary to be an effective leader. Rather, those who strive to be leaders have identified leadership qualities and figured out how to develop these qualities in themselves. The first step to becoming a leader is to be aware of the leaders around you—those people you respect, admire, and emulate—and to figure out what they do that makes others want to follow their lead.

When you analyze these leaders, you will notice that distinct and common qualities emerge. These are drive and determination to succeed, strong motivation, self-confidence, intelligence and expertise, creativity, flexibility, honesty, and integrity. Learning about these qualities will help you conduct a self-assessment and create an action plan to develop and incorporate them into your personal management style.

As you are developing your skills, it is important that you model these behaviors. You will learn how self-talk and visualization play a huge role in turning learning into habit, thinking into behavior. In life, you play many roles. How you act in each is determined by your status within any given group. Your role when parenting differs from your role when socializing with friends. It differs yet again when you see your doctor or another person you believe has greater authority and expertise. At work, your role is to be a participative, positive leader and manager.

As a manager, you are required to make many decisions. As a leader, developing your critical thinking skills will give you the ability to make wise decisions. Developing your critical thinking skills will give you the confidence to make good decisions even when you do not have the luxury of time.

When you make yourself indispensible at work, you show that you are a strong, positive, committed leader, who is willing to take risks and will always step up to the demands of your job. Staying accountable, keeping up to date on changes, looking for ways to improve, and being grateful are all ways to make yourself indispensible.

Leading your employees to perform their best makes your job easier. When you learn the steps below, you will get your employees behind you, and they will follow your lead. Becoming a strong leader is your key to success as a manager.

STEP 1: Leadership Begins with Awareness

STEP 2: Develop Positive Leadership Qualities

STEP 3: Look and Act Like a Leader

STEP 4: Critical Thinking Leads to Good Decisions

STEP 5: Make Yourself Indispensible

SPOTLIGHT ON MANAGEMENT

The Wrong Way to Lead

Alex is a newly promoted manager for a software design company. When he worked as a software engineer, his bosses were continually impressed by his knowledge and expertise. His creative ability to develop new software programs astounded everyone. All of his coworkers looked up to him. He was the go-to person when anyone had a problem, the unofficial leader of his team.

Alex now manages the six software engineers who used to be co-workers on his team. He is out of his comfort zone and has lost his self-confidence. He attended a corporate class for new managers and, although he understands his responsibilities as a manager, he has not been able to view his former coworkers as his employees.

Alex does a great job when it comes to helping his employees with problems, but even though he has a strong desire to do well, he is falling behind on meeting his corporate goals. He knows he has to do something, but he has not yet discussed goal achievement with his employees because he does not feel comfortable doing so. They all go to lunch together, but when he tried bringing it up once, he was quickly shot down by one of the guys who let him know lunchtime was not the time to talk business.

This morning, Alex's boss met with him to discuss team productivity. He pointed out that Alex's team is not where they should be in achieving yearly goals, and told him he better do something fast. Before leaving the boss's office, Alex said, "I'll see what I can do."

After the meeting, Alex commented to another manager, "Man, I'm finding out that managing is a lot different than designing. I really feel like I'm a MAC trying to be a PC in this job."

What Went Wrong?

Although Alex attended a basic management class and understands his responsibilities, feeling like a MAC trying to be a PC has left him over-whelmed and his confidence dashed. Doing a great job as a software engineer is not the same as doing a great job managing software engineers.

When Alex was promoted, the game changed. One of the reasons he was promoted was that management viewed him as a strong leader within his team. If he had worked from the start to lead through partici-pative management rather than taking a passive approach, his coworkers would have seen him in a different light. Although it would be all right to join the team for lunch once in a while, Alex continued to join the group everyday so they still considered him one of the gang.

Then, Alex lost a valuable opportunity when his boss discussed goals with him. That was the right time for Alex to open up and ask for help. When he said he would see what he could do, Alex really had no clue as to what he should do to meet the goals. Rather, he set himself up for more of the same.

Being out of his comfort zone and losing his confidence did not help. Had Alex realized that these feelings were normal for any new manager, he may have been able to rebuild his confidence rather than feeling over- whelmed.

What Could Make This Right?

First, because Alex already attended a corporate management class in which he learned basic skills, he should have analyzed his leadership and management skills. As a result, he would have been able to see areas that needed improvement and create a personal development action plan. Adding leadership development would complete his action plan.

Second, Alex needed to work on planning and organizing for him- self and his team. Writing a team plan and setting goals would have helped him understand that he was no longer one of the team, but now the team's manager. Once he had his plan and goals in place, he would have concrete items with which to confidently lead discussions with his team.

Because Alex was viewed as a leader before he was promoted, he has the necessary qualities to be a leader in his management job. The posi- tives that he has going for himself are that he already possesses some of the common qualities shared by leaders. He has a strong desire to do well. When in his comfort zone, he is self-confident and intelligent, with a high degree of job expertise and a high level of creativity.

If Alex takes the proper steps to develop his management skills and leadership qualities, he has the potential to become a positive, participa- tive leader.

STEP 1: Leadership Begins with Awareness

The question as to whether people are born leaders or can develop leadership qualities has been studied by psychologists and researchers. The case can be made for both points of view.

It is true that some people are born leaders, those few who possess charismatic personalities and an overwhelming desire to transform the world, qualities so powerful they seem to transcend the person. Examples are those people throughout history whose leadership was so outstanding that their contributions to politics, religion, science, and industry changed the world. These leaders all shared one common trait: they possessed the ability to influence a great many to pursue their goals, whether their intentions were for the good of humanity or they were motivated by evil desires.

While the vast majority of us do not possess the level of charisma that will propel us to transform the world, each of us can develop leadership qualities that will change our piece of the world. As a manager, you already possess the desire to lead. You can learn and develop the qalities you need to become the leader you want to be. It begins with awareness.

Learn Leadership Qualities

What sets leaders apart from the crowd? What special qualities do they possess ? How do they inspire others? When you analyze the leaders in your organization, family, business, and social groups, you will see that leaders possess the following qualities.

Leaders Have a Strong Desire to Achieve

Leaders have ambition and take initiative. They have high standards and challenge themselves to succeed. They are competitive. They maintain a consistently high-energy level. Leaders are positive people who want those around them to share their desire to achieve.

Leaders Are Highly Motivated

Leaders have a vision for their future and will do what needs to be done to achieve that vision. They have the ability to inspire others to believe in their goals and are able to motivate others to believe in their vision. They are risk takers, who are not afraid to take chances to achieve their goals. They do not take no for an answer. *Can't* is not part of their vocabulary. Leaders take responsibility for their mistakes, learn from them, and then move on.

Leaders Display Confidence

Leaders trust in their abilities. They strive to do their best, and they help those around them to do their best as well. They share success by giving credit to others but take full responsibility for failure. They dress for success because they know that when they look good they feel good. Leaders know how to showcase their best qualities, and they know how to do that in a quiet, humble manner.

Leaders Understand That Knowledge Is Power

Leaders have a high level of job expertise. They look for opportunities to learn, grow, and improve. They apply their critical thinking skills before they make decisions. They are problem solvers, not problem causers. Leaders balance effectiveness and efficiency by finding the right solution as quickly as they can.

Leaders Are Creative

Leaders act on their instincts. They seek out new and innovative ways to do the old. They are not afraid of the unknown, but rather embrace the new. They are interested and curious about the people, events, and environment around them. Leaders not only think outside the box, they re-create it.

Leaders Are Flexible

Leaders are resilient. When they fall, they get back up. When something goes wrong, they make it right. When life throws them a curve, they do not complain. They draw on their inner strength to solve any problem and get them through any situation. Leaders keep looking forward, not back.

Leaders Have a High Degree of Integrity

Leaders know that honesty is always the right choice. They do the right thing. They are dependable and stay true to their word. They are accountable for their actions. Leaders are trustful.

STEP 2: Develop Positive Leadership Qualities

As a frontline manager you are responsible for more than yourself; you are responsible for your employees, your customers, and your company. When you take on the responsibility of improving your leadership skills, you not only improve yourself, but also your employees, the service you provide to your customers and, ultimately, your company.

Now that you know the qualities that leaders share, you can work on personal improvement. You have already created a development plan for your management responsibilities. By adding your leadership development goals, you will complete your personal development plan.

When you work on self-development, you strengthen the positive leadership qualities you need to succeed. You probably already possess some of these qualities. You may possess some degree of all of these qualities. Even if you feel that you already are a strong, positive, participative leader, you can always find ways to strengthen and improve your skill set.

Make a List of the Common Leadership Qualities and Rate Yourself on Each

List each of the qualities from STEP 1, plus any others you feel are relevant to your role as a frontline leader. Assess your leadership qualities as you see yourself today. Make a list of your strengths and areas needing improvement.

Ask a Mentor for Help

Before you set goals, ask someone you trust to review your list. Explain that you are creating a self-development plan to strengthen your leadership abilities and would appreciate his or her input. Ask the person to be honest and open and then be receptive to the feedback you receive. Afterward, analyze the feedback and decide whether you agree and how you want to act on it.

Set Goals for Each Area of Improvement

Once you determine the qualities you need to develop and strengthen, set goals to add to your personal development plan. Be realistic about your leadership development. For major weaknesses, set step-by-step goals. Start small, but think big. Also, be realistic about expected outcomes. If you are thinking this is just another goal sheet that will create more work and take more time, look at it this way: Achieving goals will enable you to work more effectively and efficiently, and working more effectively and efficiently will ultimately give you more time.

Review Your Goals Often as a Reminder of the Qualities You Are Developing

Review your personal development plan and goals frequently. Reminding yourself how you are progressing in your leadership development will encourage you to work harder to achieve these goals. If you find that you are getting sidetracked or have gotten derailed, get back on track.

Personal development is a lifelong process. We all have some qualities and skills on which we can improve.

STEP 3: Look and Act Like a Leader

You identified the leadership qualities you want to develop. You set goals to change your behavior. Now it is time to put what you are developing into practice. The only way you will become a leader is to look and act like a leader.

Use Self-Talk to Encourage Yourself

Every morning, look in the mirror and affirm that you are a positive, participative leader. Affirmations are statements of belief, declarations of truth. To help you see yourself as a leader, begin your self-talk with present tense verbs, such as *I am* _____. Fill in the blank as appropriate—*I am strongly motivated. I am creative. I am successful. I am confident.* Stating your affirmations as positive fact will help you plant the picture of who you want to be in your mind.

Envision Yourself Already Possessing Leadership Qualities

Along with stating your affirmations, create a vision in your mind of the leader you want to be. See yourself as a positive, powerful, participative leader. Think of each leadership quality and, as you state your affirmation, picture yourself projecting the behaviors that enhance these qualities.

Dress for Success

Your appearance says a lot about you. Always dress professionally and businesslike. You are a manager and a leader, so save your casual clothes for outside of work. Even if jeans and tees are the norm for your workplace, choose ones that are dressy and fit well. Make sure you are clean and groomed at all times. This includes your hair, body, fingernails, teeth, and shoes. Remind yourself that when you look good, you feel good. And when you feel good, you will project yourself as a confident, self-assured leader.

Walk the Walk

When you are getting ready for work, get fully into your role as a powerful, participative leader. By using positive self-talk and envisioning, you are in a position to act the part. Consider that you are an actor in the play called "Work."You are playing the role of the leader. When at work, in everything you do and say, do and say it as a leader does.

STEP 4: Critical Thinking Leads to Good Decisions

Critical thinking is reflective thought about issues and situations that sometimes have no clear-cut answers or solutions. Leaders understand that critical thinking is an important skill to develop. Critical thinkers consider problems carefully before making decisions. When you learn to think critically you stay solution oriented.

Consider Each Problem Carefully

Think about the problem before you. Ask questions to clarify the situation or issue. Consider how reliable or credible your source of information is. If you need more information to make your determination, research to find out all you need to know to make an educated decision. Gather as much information from as many sources as you feel necessary before you evaluate possible solutions.

Analyze All Arguments or Proposed Solutions

Make value judgments about all possible solutions. Do not jump to conclusions before hearing all sides and gathering all information. Keep an open mind and think objectively. Do not allow your emotions to slant your thinking. Consider all possibilities and alternatives before finalizing your decision. Also, consider the impact of each proposed solution.

Decide on the Best Action

After considering all information, angles, and research, you will be able to make the right decision. Communicate your decision to all involved. If it is an unpopular decision or one that may not be well received, be sensitive to other people's feelings and explain why you decided as you did.

Be Proactive, Not Reactive

Being proactive helps you stay on top of issues before they become full-blown problems, and that makes them easier to solve. Be on the lookout for problems when they are brewing. You may not always have time on your side, so mentally practice making snap decisions to sharpen your critical thinking skills. Think about possible problems that could occur and how you would solve them. When you are proactive in using your critical thinking skills, when crises arise, or when you do not have time to carefully think out your plan of action, you will be in a better position to make quick decisions.

STEP 5: Make Yourself Indispensible

By making yourself a vital part of your organization, you make yourself indispensible. When you step up and become a positive, proactive leader, others are going to notice. When you continually strive to do your best, others are going to respect you.

Leaders Stay on Top of Their Game

Stay motivated and keep your drive and desire to be your best. Do not get stuck in a rut. Stay focused on goal achievement. Do what it takes to meet your goals. Knowledge is power, so set a goal to learn something new every day. Keep updating your development action plan to improve your skills.

Leaders Look for Opportunities to Lead the Way

Look for ways to motivate your team. When you see something done right, offer positive feedback. Look for teaching opportunities. Share your job expertise. Always try to help others succeed. When you see an opportunity to help, take responsibility and do so. Most importantly, always lead with honesty and integrity.

Leaders View Every Situation as an Opportunity

Approach every day as an adventure; every situation as an opportunity. When you do so, you will view your world from a positive perspective. Be the person others rely on and look up to. Step up and volunteer for unpopular projects. Find ways to say *yes* and *I can do that.*

Leaders Are Grateful for the People and Circumstances in Their Lives

Be thankful every day for every person and every event in your life. When you are thankful, you send out positive and uplifting messages. When you are thankful, you will feel happy. Find ways to share your gratitude and appreciation. Say *thank you.* Stay flexible and resilient. View all problems as opportunities to grow.

SPOTLIGHT ON MANAGEMENT

A Better Way to Lead

Alex is a newly promoted manager for a software design company. When he worked as a software engineer, his bosses were continually impressed by his knowledge and expertise. His creative ability to develop new software programs astounded everyone. All of his coworkers looked up to him. He was the go-to person when anyone had a problem, the unofficial leader of his team, who exuded self-confidence.

Alex now manages the six software engineers who used to be his coworkers on his team. He is out of his comfort zone and has lost his self-confidence. He attended a corporate class for new managers, and he understands his responsibilities as a manager.

After the class he analyzed his management style and realized that because he is now managing his former coworkers his style tends to be passive participative. He defined his strengths and areas needing improvement, created a development action plan, and set goals.

Alex does a great job when it comes to helping his employees with problems, but even though he has a strong desire to do well, he is falling behind on meeting his corporate goals. Yesterday he held a team meeting to discuss the problem areas, and he asked his team members for their suggestions to improve results. They started complaining and even though he felt uncomfortable, Alex took the lead and confidently told the team members that they needed to improve. Then, he asked for their commitment to achieve their goals and gained their agreement.

This morning, Alex was proactive and asked his boss to meet with him to discuss team productivity. Alex took responsibility for his team's shortcomings, told his boss about the meeting he held yesterday, showed him his goal sheet, and asked for suggestions. Alex and his boss discussed his personal development plan, and the boss suggested ways for Alex to develop his management and leadership skills.

Alex's boss told him, "The reason we promoted you was because you displayed strong leadership skills with your coworkers. I think what you're realizing now is that it's tough to separate yourself as being their manager. Let's write out some additional goals to help you develop your leadership qualities. You know, I've noticed that you've lost some of your confidence, which is quite normal considering you are out of your comfort zone. Being a new manager means finding your new comfort zone, and I'm sure that once we set goals you'll find it."

After the meeting, Alex commented to another manager, "Man, I'm finding out that managing is a lot different than designing. I really feel like I'm a MAC trying to be a PC in this job. But I'm also realizing that developing my management and leadership skills is what I need to do to get the results I want."

CHECKLIST

STEP 1: Leadership Begins with Awareness

✓ Learn leadership qualities

✓ Leaders have a strong desire to achieve

✓ Leaders are highly motivated

✓ Leaders display confidence

✓ Leaders have a high level of job expertise

✓ Leaders are creative

✓ Leaders are flexible

✓ Leaders have a high degree of integrity

STEP 2: Develop Positive Leadership Qualities

✓ Make a list of the common leadership qualities and rate yourself on each

✓ Ask a mentor for help

✓ Set goals for each area of improvement

✓ Review your goals often as a reminder of the qualities you are developing

STEP 3: Look and Act Like a Leader

✓ Use your self-talk to encourage yourself

✓ Envision yourself already possessing leadership qualities

✓ Dress for success

✓ Walk the walk

STEP 4: Critical Thinking Leads to Good Decisions

✓ Consider each problem carefully

✓ Analyze all arguments or proposed solutions

     ✓ Decide on the best action

     ✓ Be proactive, not reactive

STEP 5: Make Yourself Indispensible

     ✓ Leaders stay on top of their game

     ✓ Leaders look for opportunities to lead the way

     ✓ Leaders view every situation as an opportunity

     ✓ Leaders are grateful for people and circumstances in their lives

THE REAL WORLD

Practice Lesson

Christine, like Alex, is a newly promoted manager. As a frontline employee working for a postal services company, she was an outstanding team member. She did her job well and, as a competitive person by nature, she set high goals for herself. She sought out opportunities to help her coworkers when they had problems. Shortly before she was promoted, Christine won a company award for developing a new billing procedure.

After attending a class for new managers, she feels overwhelmed. Even though she still enjoys helping her coworkers when they have problems, Christine has difficulty figuring out how to successfully perform all of her new managerial responsibilities.

From what you learned about Christine, list which leadership qualities—strong desire to achieve, motivation, confidence, job expertise, creativity, flexibility, integrity—are her strengths.

_____

_____

_____

Next, list Christine's areas needing improvement.

_____

_____

_____

Create a development action plan for these items and set concrete goals. Keep in mind that it is difficult to set concrete goals to develop confidence (other than, say, a personal daily goal to affirm she is confident and then to envision herself behaving confidently). By setting goals for the other areas needing improvement, such as gaining job expertise in her management duties, Christine's confidence will restored as she works on her goals.

_____

_____

_____

PERSONAL PLANNER

Thoughts, ideas, and goals on your leadership skills and style:

_____

_____

_____

_____

_____

_____

_____

_____

_____

_____

_____

_____

_____

_____

_____

_____

_____

_____

_____

_____

_____

_____

_____

_____

3

Planning and Organizing for Results

You know that management involves a lot more than making sure your employees are doing their jobs correctly and productively. In addition to all the duties that come with managing others, your job also involves managing yourself and managing results. You are responsible for completing projects and other assignments, analyzing goal achievement, measuring and controlling outcomes, providing feedback, appraising employees on their performance, creating development action plans for employees, and monitoring your personal development goals. How do you keep track of all your responsibilities and keep it all straight?

Beside all your internal responsibilities, your most important role in frontline management is to ensure your customers are satisfied with the products and services you provide. How do you find the time—and the know-how—to do that?

A Customer-Focused Plan
Keeps You on the Right Track

With all the management and customer responsibilities on your plate, planning and organizing is your best chance to achieve both corporate and personal goals. Maintaining your focus on your customers when you plan and organize ensures you do the things that are important to them—and that should be the number one goal of your company.

Managing without careful planning and organizing would be like leaving for a vacation without knowing where you are going. *How will you know when you get where you're going if you haven't defined where it is you want to go?* Unless you take the time to plan your destination, know your direction, and plot your roadmap, you will never know when—or even if—you have reached your destination.

Managing with thoughtful and insightful planning is one of the most crucial aspects of your job. When you take the time to create your mission, write a plan, and establish your goals, you set yourself up for success.

The first step in planning and organizing is to create a mission statement, which is your destination. Once you know your destination, you will create your customer focused plan, which is the general direction you need to travel to reach your destination. Finally, you will write out specific goals, which is the roadmap that will move you in the right direction toward your destination.

If your company already has a master mission statement, this makes creating one for your team that much easier, as you can use it as a model to determine your team's role in achieving corporate goals. But even if your company does not have one, you can create a team mission statement by analyzing how you and your employees can contribute to your company's success.

Once you are satisfied with the vital mission statement created for your team, create your customer-focused plan. It should include each component of your mission statement, broken down and further defined to give you an overall direction to reach your destination. By including all items that are important to your mission, you will be in a position to set goals.

The only way to make sure you are moving toward your destination is to plot your roadmap by setting specific, relevant, and realistic goals.

Goal setting enables you to organize your time, talent, and resources to best achieve your mission.

Organization, to make the most of your time, is your key to getting everything done. Either you manage your time or your time manages you. Keeping a weekly and daily planner and sticking to the necessary tasks will help you keep on top of your responsibilities.

Even with thoughtful planning and organizing, everyone will be affected by stress. Sometime, something is going to happen that will unnerve you and, when it does, it can zap your energy and leave you feeling overwhelmed. Learning how to handle stress effectively will be your best defense.

You already learned that success is directly tied to how well your employees perform to give customers the best service. By following the steps below, you will be able to plan and organize how to effectively lead your employees to success.

STEP 1:   Create Your Mission Statement

STEP 2:   Create Your Customer-Focused Plan

STEP 3:   Set Goals

STEP 4:   Make the Most of Your Time

STEP 5:   Handle Stress

SPOTLIGHT ON MANAGEMENT

The Wrong Way to Plan and Organize

Lauren is a call center manager for a telecommunications company. She manages ten employees and her job responsibilities include training and developing her staff and ensuring corporate customer service goals are met.

She is required to write a yearly plan and goal sheet that tracks success in fulfilling the corporate mission. Lauren must break down each component of the mission statement and write out the contributions her team can meet. She considers this process a nuisance. After all, she already has too much to do, so she hastily puts something together, using last year's goal sheet as her model and changing a few items to keep it current.

One item that her manager makes her include on her goal sheet is to observe three contacts per employee per month, which she feels is a ridiculous objective. Thirty observations a month is almost impossible to meet because something always seems to sidetrack her when she thinks about observing her employees.

Lauren is also supposed to meet with her team to discuss the yearly plan and ways in which the members can help meet corporate goals. Although she does hold monthly meetings to share results with her employees, she does not follow through on her responsibility. She does not engage them or challenge them to improve either and, as a result, they lack the drive and vision to meet team goals. Because there is no involvement in creating the team plan, no one feels the need to take responsibility for goal achievement.

When she meets with her manager every three months to review and discuss results, often Lauren does not have the required number of observations. This causes stress because she knows her manager is going to call her on this.

What Went Wrong?

Although Lauren does write a yearly plan and goal sheet, she does not take this responsibility seriously. She views this process grudgingly, rather than seeing planning and organizing as valuable tools to achieve both her team and personal goals. She does the bare minimum when it comes to goal setting and does not clearly map out each component of the plan; therefore, she often has problems meeting her commitments, such as the thirty observations each month. She does not organize and manage her time, but rather allows her time to manage her.

What Could Make This Right?

Lauren needs an attitude adjustment. Viewing the yearly plan and goal setting as important tools would help her view her job duties differently. Holding a meeting with her employees to engage them in discussing the team plan and goals would help them feel involved and responsible. In addition, having each employee set personal goals would further their involvement and responsibility. Her manager requires her to observe three contacts for each employee each month, which Lauren feels is almost impossible. If she created a goal sheet and mapped out how many observations she needed to complete every week (or day), she would see that thirty observations was very doable when scheduled throughout the month. Moreover, creating a daily and weekly planner—and sticking to it —would help Lauren achieve her goals.

STEP 1: Create Your Mission Statement

Whether or not your company has a mission statement, you should create one for your team. Think of your mission statement as your destination. Without a specific destination in mind, it is easy to get sidetracked or lose your way completely.

A Mission Statement Is Your Overall Goal

When you get where you are going, where will you be? What is your destination? When you answer these questions, your mission will come into focus. Your mission statement represents what you stand for and what you wish to achieve. Having a team mission statement provides everyone on your team with a clear focus and, most importantly, the same focus. You may also wish to create a personal mission statement that includes your career aspirations and goals.

Analyze What Your Company, Your Team, and You Stand for

Your mission statement should be a clear representation of what your company, your team, and you expect to achieve, and it should contain clear, tangible, specific wording that describes the destination for your team (or for yourself).

Ask yourself the following questions (changing "we" to "I" as appropriate):

- Who are our customers, and how do we want them to view us?
- What services or products do we provide, and why are they important to our customers?
- What is our role in providing these services or products?
- What are the values and principles by which we operate?

When you have answered these questions and any others that are important to your work, you have the information needed to create your mission statement.

Use Your Analysis to Create Your Mission Statement

Keep it brief, keep it broad, and keep it customer focused. Remember that your mission statement is your destination. Later, you will figure out how to reach it. When writing your mission statement, think about your responsibilities and think ahead to the plan you will be creating. Make sure you include everything that is important to achieving your overall mission, and make sure that you will be able to plan and set goals to achieve each component. Here s a sample of a mission statement for Lauren's telecommunications company:

Our mission is to be our customers' provider of choice by focusing on their needs and providing cost effective products and services; by seeking new and innovative ways to improve and grow our company; and by remaining true to our values of operating morally and ethically.

From this corporate mission, Lauren can then create a team mission statement. Here is a sample:

Our mission is to do our best to provide exceptional customer service to every customer; to find innovative ways to improve our team to meet corporate goals; and always to conduct ourselves in an ethical manner.

Focus on Your Mission Daily

Everything you do should in some way move you toward achieving your mission. Post both your company and team mission statements for your team, coworkers, and customers to see. If you find that you are getting off track or busying yourself with unimportant tasks that are not tied to your mission, redirect your attention back to what is important.

STEP 2: Create Your Customer-Focused Plan

Now that you have your mission statement, what do you do with it? You fine tune and further break down each aspect of the statement to create a plan that will become your direction. Keeping a customer focus will help you find ways to do what is important to them. Your plan should include the general direction by which you will operate and manage your team to provide exceptional customer satisfaction and achieve corporate goals.

Break Down Each Aspect of Your Mission Statement

Looking at the team mission statement above, How do you achieve the goal of *providing exceptional customer service to every customer?* Specifically, what can your team do to accomplish this mission? Can you satisfy your customers 100 percent of the time? If that seems unrealistic, can you satisfy them 98 percent of the time? If you feel that is a realistic plan, then in your plan, write "We will strive to achieve 98 percent customer satisfaction on the first try."

Fine Tune All Components That Are Important to Your Plan

Now, think about how you will achieve 98 percent customer satisfaction. You might include: "Train my team on all products and services in order to find the best solution for each customer; observe my employees to make sure they are providing the best customer service; provide meaningful feedback and create development actions plans when necessary; and motivate my team to do their best." Later, you can break down each of these items to set realistic, relevant goals.

Detail All Major Work Activities on Which You Want to Concentrate

Because your mission statement is a general goal, include all of your work functions. If after reviewing the items you listed, you realize that you omitted a function, such as interviewing a random number of customers each month to determine their satisfaction after interacting with your employees. In this event, add: "interview customers after their contact with my employees to insure they are satisfied." Later, when you set goals, you can incorporate the specific number you will interview.

Review Your Plan to Make Sure It Is Challenging, Yet Achievable

Before you move into the goal setting phase, carefully review your plan. Ask: *Have I included sufficient direction to move my team—and company— toward our destination? Have I challenged myself and my team with a plan in which we can succeed? Have I incorporated all aspects of my work duties in my plan?* When you are satisfied that you have a workable plan, then you can break it down further into specific goals.

STEP 3: Set Goals

Now that you know your destination and have mapped out your general direction, the planning phase is almost complete. Next, you need to plan and organize how you will reach your destination. What specific steps do you need to take to get where you are going? Setting goals helps you organize your time, talent, and resources to set time frames to move you in the right direction.

Write Specific, Tangible, Realistic Goals

Now that you have broadened your mission into a plan, you will be able to write and organize the goals that will get you there. When you set goals, take each component you wrote in your plan and create the goals that will provide you with your roadmap.

For example, if your plan states that you will interview customers after their contact with your employees to ensure they are satisfied, how will you set a goal for this? After analyzing your work responsibilities, you may feel that you can manage interviewing four customers per employee per month.

Set Specific Time Frames

Your goal to interview four customers per employee each month is still somewhat broad. What happens when you get to the last couple days of the month and see that you have only completed one interview for each employee? By being more specific, you will find your goals are more manageable.

Look at the interview example. Let's say you have eight employees. If you work an average of twenty days a month, you will need to complete approximately eight interviews each week. Your goal may look like this: Interview four customers per employee per month by completing eight interviews per week. Is this specific? Yes. Is this tangible? Yes. Is this realistic? You have to decide. If you find that a goal you set is not doable, rewrite it. The purpose of goal setting is to keep you on the path toward your destination and to set you up for success. Setting unrealistic goals that are impossible to meet will only lead to frustration.

Break Down Large Goals into Smaller, More Manageable Ones

In your plan, you wrote that you will train your team on all products and services to achieve 98 percent customer satisfaction. By breaking down this component and writing it as step-by-step goals, you will find it easier to stay on track down the line.

You wrote your goal as: "Meet with each employee to check for understanding on products and services, determine training needs, and train all members of team by end of 1st quarter." You realize that this goal is broad and ambiguous. If you get to March and have only trained three of your employees, you may feel overwhelmed and stressed.

Breaking it down is going to make it more tangible. For example: "Meet with each employee to check for understanding on products and services by January 15. Schedule training for each employee by January 20. Complete all training by end of first quarter." Once you know your training needs, you can go back and change the goal sheet to schedule a completion date for each employee who needs additional training. For example: "Complete training as follows: Janie by January 31; Mike by February 7; Justin by February 14. . . ." Setting step-by-step goals also makes it easier if you find the need to move time frames.

Prioritize Your Goals by Importance

While all your goals should move you toward your mission, some carry more weight than others. After you prioritize your goals, review them to make sure you will be able to complete each by your committed dates.

If four interviews per employee per month is a self-imposed goal and you find that other goals are going to make this impossible to meet, change the goal to one you can achieve. Challenge yourself but stay realistic when you set goals and organize your time. Remember, you want to set yourself up for success, not doom yourself to failure.

Review Your Goals with Your Manager and Your Team

First, meet with your manager to review your goals. After agreeing on your goal plan, meet with your employees to discuss team goals. Discuss strategies to achieve the goals, and engage your employees to take responsibility for meeting them. Challenge them to set their own goals.

Periodically, Review Your Progress with Your Team

Make sure you keep them up to date on goal achievement so that they remain engaged and involved. Celebrate victories, discuss ways to overcome problem areas, and revise goals and dates if they need to be changed or updated. Goal setting is a continuous process, so when you meet your goals, set new ones.

STEP 4: Make the Most of Your Time

Now that you have your destination, direction, and roadmap, you can move your goals to your weekly planner to make sure you not only stay on the right path, but that you remain on schedule. When you organize your goals into time frames and set specific dates, you will feel confident, calm, and in control. The bottom line is that you will work more efficiently when you organize and manage your time.

Write Out a Planner, and Keep It Current

Scheduling what you plan to accomplish each day will help you accomplish more. Noting your goals on your planner puts them in your face, so to speak. Look at your goal sheet and note on your planner the tasks you need to complete and when you need to complete them.

Review Your List of Tasks Every Day

When making your daily plan, schedule a block of time at the end of the day to review and prioritize your tasks for the next day. Flexibility is most important in this step. If you find that you are getting backed up, go back to your goal sheet, rewrite your time frames, and change them on your planner. Be realistic about how much you schedule and what you can accomplish each day.

Schedule Only Three-Quarters of Your Day

Something is going to come up every day. It might be an emergency. It might be an unscheduled meeting with your boss. It might be a project assignment dropped in your lap. Or it might be that you have gotten behind on meeting a goal. Whatever the reason, you know that sometimes things just happen that you had not planned. Allowing unscheduled time every day will give you a cushion that will help you remain calm when you get hit with something unexpected.

Take Control of Your Time or Your Time Will Take Control of You

Make good use of all your time. Stick to your daily and weekly schedule as best as you can. If you frequently spend time on the telephone, make good use of hold time by filing, reading, or working on other tasks. When you call someone who is a talker, begin your conversation by telling the person that you are busy now, but you need to talk about _____. This sets the tone for the conversation and makes ending it easier.

If someone asks for help but you are busy, tell the person that you want to help but that now is not a good time. Then schedule a time that works for both of you. Learn the difference between important and urgent. Not everything is urgent.

Organize Your Workspace

An uncluttered desk and organized workspace helps you work more efficiently. Knowing where everything is located speeds up any process. When working on a task, make sure you have all necessary items within easy reach. Keep your planner up to date so that you know what tasks you need to complete. Create and organize task files to help keep your workspace clutter free; when you are done with something, put it away.

Stop Procrastinating

Make your attitude, *I'll do it now* rather than *I'll do it later.* Putting off work, especially tasks that can quickly and easily be handled at the moment, will eventually put you behind schedule. If your boss keeps assigning you additional work, and you cannot get it all done, do not procrastinate. Take the initiative and meet with him or her to discuss the situation. Bring your plan, goal sheet, and weekly planner. Rather than complaining about the additional assignments, be proactive. Tell your boss you need help in prioritizing all your work because you are finding it difficult to accomplish everything. He or she just might be surprised to see how much work you have been given and may reassign some duties.

STEP 5: Handle Stress

Even with the best planning and organization skills, things still go wrong and feelings of stress often ensue. Careful planning and organizing helps keep stress at arm's length, but depending on the circumstances, stress can overcome even the calmest person. For example, you may find that you are behind schedule in your goal of interviewing customers and your boss just dropped another project in your lap. Or, you are overscheduled with meetings this week and do not see how you can complete the employee training you had planned. Or, you just handled an upset customer, and even though you did your best to find a satisfactory solution to his problem, the way in which he spoke to you left you frazzled. Whatever the reason, stress is unavoidable.

Stress, in and of itself, is not a bad thing, but how you manage it determines whether you will move in the right direction or be derailed. When handled unsuccessfully, stress can affect both your mental and physical health. It can drain energy, causing you to become impatient, irritable and, in severe cases, depressed. It also contributes to many physical illnesses and conditions, including heart disease. Since we all encounter stress, learning how to handle it well is your best defense in keeping it under control. When you notice feelings of stress, do something about it before your health is compromised.

Get Enough Rest

This may well be your best defense to keep stress manageable. Feeling rested helps you make sound decisions, puts your critical thinking skills to good use, and enables you to work more efficiently and effectively. Contrary to the amount of sleep people think they can get by with, most of us do need around eight hours to refresh and rejuvenate our bodies. Getting enough rest—every day—is one of the best antidotes to becoming overwhelmed and stressed out.

Exercise

Exercise is a great stress reducer. While thirty to sixty minutes is a daily goal for which we should all strive, taking a ten-minute walk in the fresh air will give you a quick boost and that is often all that you need to de-stress and refresh. Just make sure you take the time to get some good exercise every day. Choose an activity you enjoy, and you are more apt to do it regularly.

Eat a Healthy Diet

Energizing your body with the right kind of fuel can help you de-stress. Eat a balanced diet, and eat in moderation. What our mothers told us was correct: breakfast is the most important meal, so start your day by fueling properly. A protein source such as a glass of milk or an egg, a whole grain such as a healthy cereal or slice of toast, and a piece of fruit will give you steady energy throughout the morning. For lunch, stay away from heavy or fried foods. Choose a healthy sandwich or a salad with meat or cheese to stay energized throughout the afternoon. When you need a pick-me-up, a high sugar snack may give you a quick boost, but when you need stamina to last the morning or afternoon, make it a wise selection, such as nuts, fruit, or yogurt.

Develop Relaxation Techniques

Deep breathing, counting to ten, getting away from a stressful situation, taking a short mental break, meditating, taking a stretch break—these are all great relaxation techniques. The best thing is that they can all be done in little time. Here are two quick relaxation techniques:

1. Close your eyes and inhale deeply. Consciously starting from your abdomen, slowly inhale to fill your lungs, hold the breath for a moment, and slowly exhale the air.

2. Close your eyes and take a quick mental vacation. Love the beach? Picture yourself feeling the warmth of the sun, breathing in the salt air, hearing the sounds of the seagulls and waves.

Learn to Be Resilient

Resiliency is one of the most important qualities you can develop to manage stressful situations. Resilient people bounce back from life's challenges, learn to overcome difficult situations, hold up under pressure, and find renewed strength in all life experiences. When life throws you a curve, put your problem-solving skills to work to find the best solution. When there is no good solution, deal with the situation to the best of your ability. Draw on your inner strength and allow family and friends to help. This will see you through the really tough times. Most importantly, try to keep your sense of humor. Laughter often can be the best medicine.

Maintain a Grateful Attitude

Appreciate the good in yourself and in others. Respect others. Be tolerant of differences. Focus on being compassionate. Walk in someone else's shoes rather than judge. Laugh. Do something fun every day. Enjoy a hobby. Count your blessings—you may be surprised by how many you really do have.

SPOTLIGHT ON MANAGEMENT

A Better Way to Plan and Organize

Lauren is a call center manager for a telecommunications company. She manages ten employees and her job responsibilities include training and developing her employees and ensuring corporate customer service goals are met.

She is required to write a yearly plan and goal sheet that tracks success in fulfilling the corporate mission. She must break down each component of the mission statement to contributions her team can meet. Although she has a busy schedule, she understands the importance of planning and organizing to achieve corporate, team, and personal goals. She also understands that writing out her goal sheet and transferring her goals to her weekly planner helps her stay on track and focused on the result.

Lauren schedules a block of time on her planner to write out her team and personal mission statements, create a customer-focused plan, and set goals. She then meets with her manager to discuss any goals that were set for her, agreeing on workable solutions to ensure that she can meet all of them. Once her meeting has finished, she transfers her goals to her planner and breaks them down by week.

Lauren also meets with her team and provides each of her employees with a copy of her yearly plan and goal sheet. Together they discuss how to achieve the goals. Lauren provides each employee with a blank goal sheet and encourages them to set their own goals and dates by which to complete each of them. She allows them time during the meeting to create their goal plans. Next, she meets individually with each employee to discuss their personal goals and how they can perform their best to help the team achieve their goals.

Lauren schedules monthly team meetings at which she shares results with the team. She celebrates successes by recognizing individual achievements and providing snacks to reward team achievements. She also uses this time to discuss problem areas and strategize how to achieve all their goals. Because of the team involvement, the members feel empowered and are committed to doing their personal best.

Quarterly, she meets with her manager to review and discuss results. Lauren comes to these meetings well prepared to talk about both achievement and areas of concern. She brings her weekly planner so her manager can see how she spends her time.

CHECKLIST

STEP 1: Create Your Mission Statement

    ✓ A mission statement is your overall goal

    ✓ Analyze what your company, your team, and you stand for

    ✓ Use your analysis to create your mission statement

    ✓ Focus on your mission daily

STEP 1: Create Your Customer-Focused Plan

    ✓ Break down each aspect of your mission statement

    ✓ Fine-tune all components that are important to your plan

    ✓ Detail all major work activities on which you want to concentrate

    ✓ Review your plan to make sure it is challenging, yet achievable

STEP 3: Set Goals

    ✓ Write specific, tangible, realistic goals

    ✓ Set specific time frames

    ✓ Break down large goals into smaller, more manageable ones

    ✓ Prioritize your goals by importance

    ✓ Review your goals with your manager and your team

    ✓ Periodically, review your progress with your team

STEP 4: Make the Most of Your Time

    ✓ Write out a planner and keep it current

    ✓ Review your list of tasks every day

    ✓ Schedule only three quarters of your day

✓ Take control of your time or your time will take control of you

✓ Organize your workspace

✓ Stop procrastinating

STEP 5: Handle Stress

✓ Get enough rest

✓ Exercise

✓ Eat a healthy diet

✓ Develop relaxation techniques

✓ Learn to be resilient

✓ Maintain a grateful attitude

THE REAL WORLD

Practice Lesson

Jeremy is a department manager for a large sporting goods store. He manages eight sales employees, and his job duties include ensuring that customers are satisfied and sales quotas are met. The corporate mission statement is:

> *Our mission is to be the number one sports and fitness retailer for all sports enthusiasts by providing our customers with all their needs and by challenging ourselves to constantly improve everything we do.*

> *It is the beginning of the year and time for Jeremy to write his team mission statement, create his plan, set goals, and organize his time.*

Write a team mission statement for Jeremy.

_____

_____

_____

Create a plan, focusing on the customer service aspect of Jeremy's mission statement.

_____

_____

_____

Set specific, relevant, and meaningful goals for this part of the plan.

_____

_____

_____

Next, move Jeremy's customer service goals for next week to his planner by noting specific tasks to be completed each day.

Monday _____

Tuesday _____

Wednesday _____

Thursday _____

Friday _____

PERSONAL PLANNER

Thoughts, ideas, and goals on planning and organizing:

_____

_____

_____

_____

_____

_____

_____

_____

_____

_____

_____

_____

_____

_____

_____

_____

_____

_____

_____

_____

_____

_____

_____

_____

PART TWO

MANAGING OTHERS

4

Communicating Up, Down, Across, In, and Out

Now that you understand your management style, learned about leadership qualities, and created a development plan, it is time to put your skills to use. We begin Part II with communication skills because many of your job functions depend on how well you communicate. Your communication skills need to be exceptional if you want to stand out as a dynamic leader. Mediocrity will not cut it.

You learned that effective leadership involves getting others to share your vision and goals. You can accomplish that by learning how to communicate well at all times by listening completely; understanding nonverbal cues; speaking your best in various situations, from informal conversations to formal presentations; mastering the art of small talk; learning how to present to an audience; and building strong relationships.

At work, you communicate to your employees, coworkers, upper management, and, also, to customers, clients, prospects, vendors, service workers, and perhaps even competitors. When you realize that every one of these people influences your outcomes and ultimately your paycheck, you begin to recognize that how you communicate to them reaps benefits directly to you. Think of it this way: when you treat everyone as though they are your valued customers, you will remember to provide exceptional service by communicating effectively to all people all the time.

Your Customers Are Everyone but You!

When you start viewing everyone as your customer, you become more service minded. You find ways to communicate in a manner that is helpful and uplifting. When you strive to provide exceptional service to everyone, you actually provide exceptional service to yourself. Compassion, concern, and care for others are returned to you through strengthened relationships. The result is that when you give great service through effective communication, others will communicate more effectively with you.

Communication is a give-and-take exchange that involves a sender and a receiver. When someone is sending a message, whether verbal or nonverbal, someone else is receiving the message. As long as the receiver is receptive to that message, it can be received properly. Use an inappropriate tone, a poor choice of words, or body language that is not in sync with your message, and the receiver may misinterpret your intent or tune you out completely. By improving your skills, both as the sender and the receiver, you become a great communicator and increase your chances of managing and leading effectively.

As a manager, you communicate for a variety of reasons. You ask and answer questions, seek and provide information, conduct and attend meetings, interview, negotiate, train, make presentations, and often communicate informally by making small talk, which offers an opportunity for people to get to know you better. When you develop your communication skills, you present yourself well no matter the circumstance, no matter the person.

The most important component of communicating is listening. Unless you listen completely, you will not know how to respond appropriately or accurately. When you pay attention to the speaker, refrain from judging, keep your emotions in check, and clarify for understanding before responding, you show the speaker that his or her message is important to you.

Nonverbal communication makes up a large portion of communication. When you convey a pleasant facial expression, maintain a relaxed and open demeanor, project confidence, and are mindful of your gestures, you make it easier for your messages to be understood correctly. Likewise, by paying attention to the speaker's nonverbal communication, you can better understand the emotions behind the message you are receiving.

When you send a message, remember that once sent a message cannot be taken back. Therefore, think before you speak. Communicating clearly and precisely, using good grammar, matching your tone to the message, asking questions and responding appropriately, and incorporating powerful, positive words in your message will enhance communication.

In your management role, you have many opportunities to make small talk, which is an important component of business communication. Whether you are attending a conference, a meeting, a luncheon, a social gathering, or conversing with your employees and coworkers in your workplace, small talk is a big factor in how positively others perceive you. It is often a factor for consideration in promotions. Keeping up to date on current events, understanding that certain topics are taboo, learning how to pick up on others' cues, and having the ability to ask and answer questions and relate interesting anecdotes will help you master the art of small talk.

You also have many instances where you will make presentations. You may be asked to train a group of employees, conduct a meeting, or give a formal speech to a large group. Knowing your audience and the purpose of your presentation, developing and preparing your material, and practicing your talk will help you gain confidence and manage your nerves.

Building and maintaining strong relationships is necessary to your career development. You are in a position to form relationships with many people, including the employees who report to you, your coworkers, your boss, upper management, a mentor, vendors, and other outside contacts, as well as customers. Finding common ground, taking the time to get to know people, being genuinely interested in others, making people feel valued, and being viewed as a good friend help you build and maintain relationships.

When you practice the steps below, you will be on your way to mastering the art of communicating well with anyone at any time.

STEP 1: Listen Well

STEP 2: Communicate Well Nonverbally

STEP 3: Speak Well

STEP 4: Learn the Art of Small Talk

STEP 5: Learn the Art of Presentations

STEP 6: Maintain Strong Relationships

SPOTLIGHT ON MANAGEMENT

The Wrong Way to Communicate

Stephanie is a department manager for a large department store chain. She has been a frontline manager just under a year and feels good about the progress she is making on her personal development plan. She has attended some management classes, and today is the first day of a week-long sales management training conference. Because this is a corporate-wide conference, she will have the opportunity to meet and mingle with people she does not know. She is not looking forward to it.

Stephanie has worked hard to overcome her shyness, and she feels comfortable when talking to her employees or manager, but attending classes and conferences where she does not know the other attendees leaves her feeling uncomfortable and ill at ease. Making small talk is not easy for her and even the thought of walking into a room of strangers leaves her with a feeling of dread.

She signed in, picked up her name tag, took a deep breath, and walked into the room where coffee and breakfast were being served. Stephanie did not make eye contact with anyone. She filled her plate, poured a cup of coffee, and found an empty table. As she sat quietly, listening to the chatter and laughter in the room, she noticed that other people were taking the time to get to know each other.

What Went Wrong?

Even though Stephanie felt proud about overcoming her shyness, those old feelings of insecurity probably still arise when she is out of her comfort zone. She allowed her feelings of discomfort and dread to surface when she entered the breakfast room. Then, when she did not make eye contact and introduce herself and when she sat alone, she alienated herself from the group. Sitting alone, listening to the chatter and laughter, most likely made her feel even more isolated and heightened her feelings of insecurity.

What Could Make This Right?

Stephanie needs to learn the art of small talk. A little practice and preparation beforehand would have helped a great deal in overcoming her feelings of awkwardness and shyness. She could have prepared some work related-questions in advance, read the newspaper and picked out an interesting story, or thought of a funny anecdote about her workplace to share. Practicing her introduction and opening questions in a mirror prior to walking into the room would have helped calm her nervousness. Then, when she walked into the breakfast room, smiling warmly and making eye contact would have helped her gain confidence. Picking out someone to whom to introduce herself would have helped her break the ice. She could then open with a conversation starter question, such as

"What store do you work in?" or "How long have you been a manager?," which would get the other person talking.

STEP 1: Listen Well

Effective managers and leaders know that listening actively and completely is the only way they will hear a message and be able to respond correctly. When you listen, people respond. When you do not listen, people know.

Tune Out, Tune In

Unless you communicate in a vacuum, it is easy to get sidetracked when there are outside stimuli, such as people coming and going, other people's conversations, or loud noises that make it difficult to hear. When you tune out distractions and tune in by paying complete attention to the speaker, you are in a better position to hear the correct message. Do not allow your mind and thoughts to stray. If they do, bring your full attention back to the speaker.

Stay Involved

In face-to-face siuations, keep your eyes on the speaker. Do not allow your eyes to wander; doing so sends the message that you are more interested in what is going on around you than in the speaker. Smile, laugh, show concern, or remain passive, as is appropriate to the message. If the message is long, show the speaker you are listening actively by nodding from time to time, saying something like *I see,* or asking a question such as *What happened next?* Similarly, when on the phone, keep your attention on the speaker and do not look around.

Keep an Open Mind

When you are listening, do not interrupt. Remain objective and do not judge or jump to conclusions. Wait until you hear the entire message before making an evaluation. Further, because it is easy to get caught up in the emotions of the speaker, especially if you are personally invested, keep your feelings in check and do not let emotional words or topics cause you to react impulsively or inappropriately.

Check for Understanding

When the speaker is finished and before you respond, think about what you heard and make sure you understood the message correctly. Put your critical thinking skills to good use and rephrase the speaker's main points in your own words or, if you are confused, ask questions to clarify before moving on.

STEP 2: Communicate Well Nonverbally

Effective managers and leaders know that a major part of communicating with others is not what they say, but rather how they look and act. Words and actions do not always match, and it is the actions that convey the emotions behind spoken words. Feelings and emotions are reflected outward and picked up through facial expressions, body movement and posture, gestures, and personal space. Your body language sends a message; likewise, you receive a message through the body language of the person speaking to you.

Watch Your Facial Expressions

Your face can be a snapshot of your attitude and emotions, so make sure your facial expressions match the message. Show happiness, excitement, concern, sadness, shock, or passivity, depending on the message you are sending or receiving. Making eye contact shows that you are interested, so whether you are speaking or listening, use eye contact effectively, but not excessively. A smile communicates in any language and culture, signaling warmth and friendliness, so smile as often as appropriate. When remaining passive, keep a pleasant facial expression that conveys openness and interest.

Watch Your Body Movement and Posture

Maintain a relaxed, open demeanor. Stand or sit up straight without appearing rigid, hold your head high, and maintain good posture. Keep your arms in a relaxed position at your sides with your hands open or fold your hands in front of you. When you do these things, you project confidence. Face the person with whom you are communicating to show respect. In addition, make sure that when in a group, you do not stand in front of or block another person from seeing the speaker.

Watch Your Gestures

Gestures can enhance communication by adding interest and expressiveness, as long as they are not used excessively or exaggeratedly. When gesturing with your hands, allow your gestures to flow naturally. When gestures are too exaggerated, people will focus more on your movements than on what you are saying.

Watch Your Space

Every person has a personal "space," the distance they feel comfortable in relationship to nearness to others. Stand too close and you invade another's space and can make them feel uncomfortable or threatened. Stand too far away and you may appear distant and unapproachable. As a rule, two feet apart is an average distance for personal space. Pay attention to the body language of the person with whom you are communicating. That will tell you whether you are too close or far away.

STEP 3: Speak Well

Effective managers and leaders know that every time they speak, whether it is a formal presentation or an informal chat with an employee, people pay close attention to what they have to say and how they say it. You are in control of the conversation, as long as what you are saying is receptive to listeners. How you deliver a message is critical to being understood correctly and communicating effectively.

Think Before You Speak

There is no communication rule more important to remember than to think first, speak second. Words are like arrows: once spoken, they take flight and cannot be taken back. Say the wrong words and you can cause someone to feel hurt, angry, upset, disheartened, or confused. Always opt for words that are uplifting and show that you value and respect others. If you feel it will help you communicate more effectively, write down key points that you want to include in your message. Before sharing any information, check your information for accuracy. And never ever gossip.

Be Specific

When sending a message, opt for the fewest and easiest words possible to get your message across correctly and completely. Speak clearly and precisely. When delivering a long message, pay attention to make sure your listener is staying with you. If not, stop and rephrase what you are saying or ask a clarifying question before proceeding.

Use Good Grammar

Always practice good grammar, whether you are at work or outside of work. Choose yes rather than yeah. Drop clichés and other overused phrases from your vocabulary. Profanity may be offensive, so make it a habit to never use it. Your listener may not understand jargon, slang, text shortcuts, or technical terms, so stick with conventional language.

Ask Good Questions

Use open-ended questions when you need to gather information and closed questions when you need additional information or to clarify answers. When listening to a person's reply, keep an open mind and make sure you are on the same page before proceeding. If you need to ask a series of questions, explain why you are doing so to help the other person be receptive. If it will help, prepare your questions in advance.

Incorporate Positive Words

Use powerful, positive words whenever you can, such as: *Absolutely; Yes; I'll be happy to; Let's try it; Sounds great* . . . you get the idea. When you need someone to do something, it always comes across more positively when you ask rather than tell: *Will you?* rather than *You will.* When suggesting a person do something, say *you could* rather than *you should.* Remember basic courtesies: *please, thank you, you're welcome, I'm sorry.* And when you know a person's name, use it during the conversation: *I'll be happy to do that, Janet.*

Time Your Message

Analyze the situation before launching into a conversation. Now might not be the right time. And if it is not, your message will either be ill received or not received at all. If you are unsure, ask the person if it is a good time to talk. If not, schedule a time when it will be.

STEP 4: Learn the Art of Small Talk

Effective managers and leaders know that small talk, or informal conversation, is critically important in their jobs. Small talk is used to break the ice with people you do not know, to start conversations when you are in unfamiliar settings, to get to know someone, or to fill time. When you learn how to use small talk to your advantage, you come across as a confident, interesting person.

Stick to Safe Topics

Generally, weather, current events, sports, entertainment, and shared commonalities are safe topics. Definitely off limits are inquiring about or sharing overly personal information, religion, and politics. By keeping up on current events, you will always have topics to begin a conversation.

Be Prepared with a Few Conversation Starter Questions

Always be prepared with some safe topic questions that you can use to open a conversation. *What did you think about that game last night? Have you seen the movie _____? How long have you worked here? How do you know Cathy?* When you ask a conversation starter question, listen closely to the answer so that you can keep the conversation going. No matter what, do not get involved in any heated debates. Be mindful of the person with whom you are speaking and steer away from or change the topic when emotions get heated.

Be Prepared to Share Something About Yourself

If you are attending an event, such as a conference or a business social event, look at these gatherings as public relations opportunities. Think of ways to promote yourself and your accomplishments without coming across as arrogant or boastful. Relating a personal work-related anecdote is a great ice breaker that may also be a lead in for sharing your accomplishments. For example, *You wouldn't believe the call I received from a new client yesterday.* Consider that people want to get to know you, so think of questions others might ask and how you will respond. When possible, respond with more than one or a couple words. Answer in a way that will keep the conversation going.

Practice Before the Event

Whenever you attend an event with people you do not know, view it as an opportunity to get to know others and for them to get to know you. Having a conversation with yourself beforehand may seem silly but it will help you feel more comfortable during the event. Ask questions, relate something interesting about yourself, and respond to likely questions. Always use positive words when practicing small talk and remember to visualize yourself interacting well with others.

Relax and Be Yourself

Think about the nonverbal communication cues you learned in STEP 2. At these events, people are going to pick up on your cues. By preparing and practicing before any event (even if the event is walking into a meeting you frequently attend), you will gain confidence to use small talk to your advantage and you will be viewed as a warm, friendly, interesting person to whom others gravitate. Be the first to say hello. Be the first to ask a question. Knowing yourself, preparing, and practicing will help you increase your comfort level in any small talk situation.

STEP 5: Learn the Art of Delivering a Presentation

Effective managers and leaders know how to come across positively and confidently when delivering a presentation. But let's face it: most people dread the thought of giving a formal presentation. Conducting a training session with your employees may leave you feeling as terrified as delivering a speech to a large group of strangers.

Know Your Audience

To whom will you be presenting? Once you identify your target audience, you will be able to create an effective, meaningful presentation. What is the purpose of the presentation? Think about your presentation from your audience's perspective. What do you want your audience to gain from your presentation?

Prepare Your Material

Now that you have identified your audience and purpose, you can begin to organize your thoughts. Research your topic until you are satisfied that you have sufficient information. This will give you the confidence to come across as a well-informed expert. Create an outline of the main points you want to cover in your presentation. Talk through it to make sure your outline flows logically from point to point. Edit until you are comfortable with the format of your presentation. When you are satisfied with your basic outline, think of some stories, anecdotes, and examples to interject throughout the presentation to make it more appealing and interesting to your listeners. In particular, you want to immediately draw your audience in, so create a powerful opening. Likewise, you want your audience to remember your speech so create a powerful closing.

Practice Your Presentation

The more you practice the more comfortable you will feel with your material. The more comfortable you feel with your material, the more confident you will be delivering your presentation. Confidence is a powerful tool, because your audience will feel your positive energy. When you practice, make good use of your outline and notes but do not read your speech. Practice varying your tone, inflection, pitch, and speed. Tape yourself to hear how you sound. When you are satisfied with how you sound, practice in a mirror and pay attention to your body language and facial expressions. Practice making eye contact, switching your gaze from one person to another in a pace that is comfortable, not staged.

Look Good

Before the presentation, select an outfit that you will feel comfortable wearing and make sure it is clean, pressed, and has "no strings attached," meaning that hems and other seams are in good repair. Check your shoes to make sure they are shined and in good condition. Before your presentation, check yourself carefully in the mirror to make sure you look your best. When you know you look good, you will feel good.

Manage Your Pre-Presentation Nerves

Practice may not make perfect, but it will help you gain confidence and feel more assured. Still, it is completely normal to feel nervous before delivering a presentation. Once you learn how to channel your nervousness into positive energy, you will welcome the pre-speech jitters. Take slow, deep breaths before you begin. Remind yourself of the importance of the material you are presenting. As you speak, focus on the members of the audience and the material you are presenting rather than on yourself.

Engage the Group

Try to involve the audience by asking a question to which they can call out answers. This can be done at the beginning of your presentation or during your talk. If your presentation is lengthy, schedule short breaks frequently, even if it is a quick stand and stretch break. Stay on time by using your notes and outline, but also be mindful of your audience and whether they are staying with you. Find the balance between speaking so slowly that people become bored or so quickly that your audience does not have time to process what you are saying. The most important thing to remember whenever you present material is to make it a positive, fun experience, both for you and for your audience.

STEP 6: Maintain Strong Relationships

Effective managers and leaders know that when they communicate effectively, they can develop close relationships. In your management position, you have opportunities to develop relationships with the employees who report to you, your coworkers, your boss, upper management, a mentor, coworkers, and outside contacts, as well as customers. You already know you cannot do it alone; you need to get others on your side to get the job done. When you take the time to cultivate relationships, you will never be alone.

Find Common Ground

The first step in building a relationship is to find something you share in common with another person. Use the skills you learned in mastering the art of small talk to establish a rapport by smiling, asking a question, sharing something about yourself, and being receptive and open. When you find something you share in common, you can begin to build on that commonality to start developing a relationship.

Be Genuinely Interested in Others

When you invest the time to get to know someone, you show that you are interested. Being friendly and open, listening well, picking up on the other person's emotions, and responding appropriately indicate that you are interested. When you are truly interested in someone, you demonstrate that you are willing to invest the time and energy to develop a relationship.

Make People Feel Valued

Think about the type of people you enjoy spending time with. Most likely, they are people who build you up, rather than wear you down. In the beginning of this chapter, you read that your customers are everyone but you. When you form this mindset, you will stay service focused. When you stay service focused, you look for ways to make other people's lives better. Always try to instill positive feelings in others and show that you appreciate and value them.

Be a Good Friend

Friends stay true. They are honest and trustworthy. They are dependable. They are sensitive and respectful of other people's feelings and situations. They step up, pitch in, and help out—without being asked. They believe in their friends and do what they can to make their lives better. Sometimes they just offer an ear or a shoulder and nothing more. They appreciate their friends. They forgive them when they do something wrong. When you think about these qualities, you can apply them to any relationship, whether it is a personal or a work acquaintance.

Strengthen Relationships

All relationships require continual maintenance. If you do not work to strengthen your relationships, you run the risk of taking others for granted. When you do that, the other person may feel resentful and unappreciated. As a result, communication may break down. So to keep your relationships strong, always focus on common ground, stay genuinely interested, make the other person feel valued, and be a good friend.

SPOTLIGHT ON MANAGEMENT

A Better Way to Communicate

Stephanie is a department manager for a large department store chain. She has been a frontline manager just under a year and feels good about the progress she is making on her personal development plan. She has attended some management classes and today is the first day of a week-long sales management training conference. Because this is a corporate wide conference, she will have the opportunity to meet and mingle with people she does not know.

Stephanie has worked hard to overcome her shyness and feels comfortable when talking to her employees or manager, but attending classes and conferences where she does not know the other attendees leaves her feeling uncomfortable and ill at ease. Making small talk is not easy for her and even the thought of walking into a room of strangers can leave her with a feeling of dread.

Because she understands the importance of small talk to her career development, Stephanie keeps up on current events by reading the newspaper and online news sources. She also pays attention to sports and entertainment news. Before attending this conference, she prepared a list of conversation starter questions about recent news events, a book she just finished, and the summer blockbuster movies that are coming out. In addition, she wrote some work-related questions and thought of a couple interesting anecdotes she could share about herself.

This morning, before going down for the pre-conference breakfast, Stephanie practiced asking questions, responding to questions, and talking about herself.

She signed in, picked up her name tag, took a deep breath, paused at the doorway of the room to survey the situation, and noticed some of the attendees were awkwardly standing alone. Then she walked right up to a stranger, smiled, and said, "Hi my name is Stephanie Walker."

"Hi Stephanie, I'm Julie Bowers."

"What store do you work in?" Stephanie listened to Julie's reply, and continued their conversation.

"Have you eaten yet?" She asked.

"No, I haven't, but I'm starved."

"Why don't we get some food before they call us into the meeting?" They filled their plates, and Stephanie led the way to a partially occupied table.

"Good morning. May we join you?" They were welcomed and joined in the table conversation. Because she immediately broke the ice, came prepared to take part in conversations, and started developing a relationship with others, Stephanie felt comfortable and relaxed when they moved to the conference room.

CHECKLIST

STEP 1: Listen Well

    ✓ Tune out, tune in

    ✓ Stay involved

    ✓ Keep an open mind

    ✓ Check for understanding

STEP 2: Communicate Well Nonverbally

    ✓ Watch your facial expressions

    ✓ Watch your body movement and posture

    ✓ Watch your gestures

    ✓ Watch your space

STEP 3: Speak Well

    ✓ Think before you speak

    ✓ Be specific

    ✓ Use good grammar

    ✓ Ask good questions

    ✓ Incorporate positive words

    ✓ Time your message

STEP 4: Learn the Art of Small Talk

    ✓ Stick to safe topics

    ✓ Be prepared with a few conversation-starter questions

    ✓ Be prepared to share something about yourself

    ✓ Practice before the event

    ✓ Relax and be yourself

STEP 5: Learn the Art of Delivering a Presentation

- ✓ Know your audience
- ✓ Prepare your material
- ✓ Practice your presentation
- ✓ Look good
- ✓ Manage your pre-presentation nerves
- ✓ Engage the group

STEP 6: Maintain Strong Relationships

- ✓ Find common ground
- ✓ Be genuinely interested in others
- ✓ Make people feel valued
- ✓ Be a good friend
- ✓ Strengthen relationships

THE REAL WORLD

Practice Lesson

Chad enjoys his job managing a team of call center reps for an insurance company. He recently received a district award for creating a framework of questions for his reps to follow when answering calls. It was so helpful and well received that his district manager would like the framework adopted for company-wide use. He asked Chad to give a presentation at the quarterly operations meeting where all upper management, including corporate officers, will be in attendance. Chad, of course, said yes!, and was thrilled to be recognized, but immediately after hanging up felt nervous and dreaded the thought that he committed to this. The meeting is scheduled in two weeks.

Help Chad prepare for his presentation. Identify the audience. Write down the purpose of his presentation and what he hopes his audience will gain from it.

_____

_____

_____

What steps should Chad take to prepare for his presentation?

_____

_____

_____

After Chad is comfortable with his preparation, what does he need to do next?

_____

_____

_____

Write down some ways that Chad can engage the attendees, keeping in mind that he is presenting to his superiors. Include a powerful opening and closing question or statement.

_____

_____

_____

_____

_____

_____

_____

_____

PERSONAL PLANNER

Thoughts, ideas, and goals on communication skills:

_____

_____

_____

_____

_____

_____

_____

_____

_____

_____

_____

_____

_____

_____

_____

_____

_____

_____

_____

_____

_____

_____

_____

_____

_____

_____

5

Training for Excellence

Training for excellence reaps big rewards. Your employees perform their best. You get results and reach your goals. Whether you are asked to conduct a training session in a classroom setting, train a new employee on the job, show a coworker how to perform a task, demonstrate a new procedure during a meeting, or bring an employee up to speed on a new practice, training effectively and thoroughly is the only way to achieve all your goals.

How effectively you train determines how effectively your employees will learn. When you take adequate time to prepare the training material on technical job skills and customer service and when you know how best to present it, you set your team and yourself up for success. Consider that the more you train, the better trainer you will become; the more you train, the better your employees will perform.

The Only Way to Satisfy Customers Is to Know HOW to Satisfy Them!

Well-trained employees are your access key to achieving your goals. When your employees are fully trained, they will know what to do, when to do it, and how to do it—and that is the only way they can perform their best. What you expect is what you are going to get. When you invest the time to train, you earn the right to expect the best and to set the bar high.

Effective training begins by knowing who needs what training, so the first step is to analyze the training needs of your team. Because learners are not one size fits all, understanding how each employee learns best will help you plan the most effective delivery method.

After analyzing your needs and your employees' learning styles, determine the most effective means of conducting the training. Ensuring that you know your material thoroughly, selecting the best delivery method, choosing the location, and scheduling the time frames are all important considerations.

Training employees to do their jobs includes training in the technical aspects of their duties, company policies and procedures, and customer relations. This will teach them to give each customer the level of service he or she deserves. In addition, team members will perform their jobs better if they understand the big picture, meaning what other departments do and how they interact with yours. Following up after any training will ensure that employees are using new skills correctly.

Finally, the training chapter covers how to conduct meetings because meetings offer training and teaching opportunities. Opening, leading, controlling, understanding group dynamics, and closing your meetings effectively will enable you to conduct meetings that your employees and coworkers will view as productive and worthwhile.

When you practice the steps below, you will be on your way to mastering the art of training for excellence.

STEP 1: Understand Learning Styles

STEP 2: Prepare for Training Sessions

STEP 3: Train Thoroughly

STEP 4: Follow Up after Training

STEP 5: Conduct Productive Meetings

SPOTLIGHT ON MANAGEMENT

The Wrong Way to Train

Kimberly works for a casual dining restaurant chain, managing the dining room wait staff. Last week she attended a half day "train-the-trainer" class for a new order input computer program that all her servers need to learn. She felt the material was easy to grasp and had no problems understanding the new system. The program was implemented yesterday, so she scheduled her employees to come in thirty minutes before the restaurant opened to receive their training. She played the training DVD, but because it lasted almost thirty minutes there was no time for questions.

The evening was a disaster. Kimberly spent the entire time at the computer terminal answering questions, retraining her employees, and dealing with their frustrations. She provided five free meals for diners who were upset when their orders were input incorrectly and she tried, unsuccessfully, to appease one diner who angrily said he would never be back. Then, when some of the dining staff complained to the kitchen staff, those employees started griping about orders coming back. The kitchen manager became angry and had words with Kimberly about her team's lack of understanding of the new program.

By evening's end, Kimberly was completely frazzled. She spent this morning at work completing the administrative duties she had no time to work on last night. She is upset with her employees and feels they did not take the training seriously. She plans to tell them how disturbed she is when they come to work this afternoon.

What Went Wrong?

Since Kimberly found the training easy to comprehend, she assumed her staff would as well. By not taking time to analyze her employees' learning styles, Kimberly overestimated the effectiveness of merely playing a DVD for her team. Then, when she did not provide any hands-on training or time for questions and group discussion, she had no way of knowing how well her employees understood the material. Since the responsibility to train fell on Kimberly's shoulders, she should be upset with herself rather than with her employees.

What Could Make This Right?

Since Kimberly was training her entire staff, incorporating all three learning styles—visual, auditory, and tactile—would have ensured that each employee grasped the training. For example, she could have played the DVD, led a group discussion and answered questions, and demonstrated the order input system on the computer. Training in this manner would have cleared up any questions and confusion. Thus, although there still would have been a learning curve that evening, frustration would have been reduced. Finally, including a discussion on the impact of the new system on customer satisfaction would have helped. She could have asked her employees to educate customers about the new system and to inform them that the ordering process might be a little slower than usual. Keeping customers "in the know" can go a long way to increasing their understanding when things go wrong.

Finally, good training leads to increased job satisfaction levels, which can increase employee retention. Kimberly should reevaluate her training methods and look for training opportunities. Frustrated employees are often the first to jump ship, and right now her employees most likely are feeling very frustrated.

STEP 1: Understand Learning Styles

People learn in different ways. An approach that works well with one employee may leave another feeling frustrated. The three distinct learning styles are visual, auditory, and tactile. Knowing which style fits each of your attendees will help you plan productive training sessions. In cases where you do not know your attendees well, combining all three styles will increase their ability to grasp the material.

Visual Learners Learn by Seeing

These employees are "let-me-see-it" learners, who retain well when they read or see the material. These learners easily understand training manuals, graphs, handouts, diagrams, and visual aids. They do well in independent environments where they set their own pace, while they may become bored in classroom settings if the pace moves too slowly.

Auditory Learners Learn by Listening

These employees are "tell-me" learners, who thrive in classroom settings. Lectures and class discussions are effective training tools. Group reading out loud and listening to tapes are both effective methods for presenting material. They may have difficulty grasping printed material.

Tactile Learners Learn by Doing

These employees are "show-me" learners, who need a hands-on experience. On-the-job-training works best for them. Touching and doing an activity is important. Demonstrate the task, and then have them demonstrate it. Tell them what to say, and then have them say it. This style is effective for most people, so try to incorporate this method into any training opportunity.

People Learn Best When Material Flows Logically

Whatever method you employ, material that moves seamlessly and systematically from one step to the next will help your attendees understand the material. When planning your training sessions, go through the material as if you were an attendee to make sure it flows well.

Incorporate All Three Learning Styles When Possible

When you do not know your employees' learning styles or your group consists of a combination of all types, the most effective training method is to vary activities to incorporate all three styles. Have the members of your team read alone and then take turns reading aloud. Lecture, then allow time for group discussion and question-and-answer activities. Demonstrate with hands-on activities to bolster understanding for all employees.

Eliminate Distractions from Training

In any training environment, outside factors can cause people to lose focus. Think of factors that can be bothersome for your employees. Noise can be distracting when it interferes with a person's ability to concentrate. Physical discomfort can be distracting, particularly if attendees must sit for a long period of time on uncomfortable chairs or in a cramped space that is too hot or too cold. Lighting can be a distraction if it is too dim for reading or so bright that it causes learners to squint.

STEP 2: Prepare for Training Sessions

As you know, planning before you begin any activity will build your confidence and increase your effectiveness. Before jumping into any training, you should identify your specific training needs. Who needs training? What kind do they need? These questions are easy to answer for new employees or when you are training a new procedure, but it is still wise to analyze where each employee is in the development process so you will know specifically who needs what. Planning before you begin any type training will enable you to target and tailor your training to both your employees' needs and the needs of your business.

Determining Your Training Needs

For teaching formal material, the "what" and "who" are already answered. If you are identifying what additional technical, policy and procedure, and customer service training is needed, analyze your employees' personal development plans.

Plan Your Delivery Method

No matter whether you are conducting a formal training class, leading a self-paced session, or providing on-the-job training to an employee, you will be more effective when you plan all aspects of your training.

Here are some general training tips:

- ✓ Instructor led—Vary your delivery by reading out loud, having attendees take turns reading out loud, and reading to themselves; following up with group discussions, brainstorming exercises, and question-and-answer periods; and incorporating fun activities, such as games, role play, or competitions.

- ✓ Self-paced—Before beginning, briefly review the material with attendees; check on them periodically; tell them what to do if they run into a problem; and follow up with discussion, allowing time to answer questions.

- ✓ On-the-job—Keep distractions to a minimum; demonstrate, then allow the employee to perform the task; make sure the employee understands the task before moving on; and follow up with discussion, allowing time to answer questions.

- ✓ General—Schedule short breaks frequently; take stretch breaks; pass out a piece of candy for an afternoon pick-me-up; and change or alternate activities frequently.

Prepare Yourself for Training

Whenever and however you train, establish a relaxed, open atmosphere by maintaining a positive attitude, keeping focused on the material, staying relaxed, encouraging student participation, and focusing on the goals. Write an introduction to begin your training. Whether you tell a story, ask a question, or begin with a warm-up exercise, make these first few minutes interesting. Keep your introduction short and stick to the basics.

Explain the purpose for the training and discuss learning objectives. And, always remember to practice beforehand.

Establish Time Frames for Training

Think about your hours of operation, busy periods, and employee coverage. Create a schedule to which you can conform. When you make employee training a priority, your employees will make it their priority.

Choose the Right Location

Select a setting that is conducive to training. Whether the session is instructor led or self-paced, find a suitable room or area. If you are training a group, a U-shaped rectangular or round table works well. Learners can face each other for discussions, and you can move easily within and around the group. If your employees are expected to work independently, find a desk or table for them to complete the material. For on-the-job training, find a location where traffic and noise will be minimal.

STEP 3: Train Thoroughly

Training thoroughly means providing your employees and coworkers with the necessary tools to do their jobs. The only way you can expect excellence is by training for excellence. Being fully trained in products, services, and company policies will enable everyone on your team to find the right solution for each customer.

Train on Technical Skills

When analyzing what and whom you need to train, consider that employees will perform most capably if they know how to find the right solution for each customer. Take sufficient time to train employees on products, services, and other technical skills. Before allowing employees to interact with customers, make sure they have the necessary tools to achieve this goal.

Training on Company Policy and Procedures

Train your employees about how company policies and procedures apply to customer interactions. Teach them to solve problems and make good decisions. In addition, tell them how far they can go to satisfy a customer and at what point you should be involved in such decisions. Further, you might consider training your team on the big picture; that is, what other departments do and how they impact and interact with your team.

Train on Customer Relations

Once your employees have completed their technical training, spend time teaching them on how to interact with customers.

This includes:

✓ Making a great first impression by smiling, making eye contact, maintaining an open and relaxed demeanor, keeping facial expressions friendly, dressing appropriately, and being properly groomed.

✓ Projecting a positive attitude by being helpful, interested, trustworthy, reassuring, respectful, and reliable.

✓ Communicating effectively by listening completely, speaking courteously and clearly, using correct grammar, asking the right questions and appropriately answering customers' questions, and making each customer feel valued.

✓ Building relationships by greeting each customer, finding the best solution to any problems, and making sure each customer is satisfied.

✓ Specific steps you expect your employees to take when interacting with customers, such as greeting them, helping them, handling problems, and understanding when to escalate situations to your attention.

STEP 4: Follow Up After Training

When training is completed, your job is not yet done. How will you know if your employees really grasped the material? How will you know they are performing as trained? And, what if they are not able to employ their new skills right away? The only way you will answer these questions is to follow up with them after the training.

Spend Time with Attendees Afterward

Observe how they apply the skills you taught. Listen when they speak to customers. Watch how they interact. Sit with them, and observe their work. Pay attention to all details. Ask questions to make sure they have the correct understanding. Correct behaviors before bad habits form.

Look for Teaching and Training Opportunities

Keep in mind that the more you train people, the better trainer you will become. The better trainer you become, the better your employees will be equipped to handle any customer situation. Always look for opportunities to help employees and coworkers improve their skills. If you see someone behave incorrectly, train immediately if it will be a quick fix. If it is an employee, say something like, *Let me show you how I would like you to do that.* If it is a coworker, try, *I've found a better/easier/quicker way to do that. Mind if I show you?* For a task that will require in-depth training, schedule a time when you can get together. Use the learning method that works best, but if you are undecided, incorporate all three styles.

Train Employees to Conduct Market Research

As direct links to your customers, your employees are in the best position to conduct market research. Train them to pay attention when customers give feedback. In addition, teach them to ask key questions, such as *What else can I do for you?* or *Is there anything else we should be doing?* When they listen to what customers tell them and then relate both positive and negative comments to you, you will have a good idea of how well you are satisfying all your customers.

Training Is Continual

Learning never stops; neither should training. When you look for and act on training opportunities, you improve the skills of your employees and coworkers and make it easier for customers to do business with you. Well-trained employees translate into satisfied customers. Be a good teacher. Tell, show, demonstrate, help, stand behind, nudge, and offer encouragement.

STEP 5: Conduct Productive Meetings

Meetings have many purposes and frequently offer training opportunities. Whenever you conduct a meeting, look for an opportunity to train. It might be as simple as sharing the terrific way one of your employees handled a customer. It might be explaining a new procedure one of your coworkers suggested. Or it might be clearing up confusion on a procedure. Running meetings effectively and efficiently will make you stand out as a dynamic leader who looks for ways to make things better.

Plan Purposeful Meetings

Surely you have been to meetings that were time wasters: those that lasted too long, did not follow the agenda, and allowed too much discussion. Those where the leader did not maintain control, or those where you came away wondering why you were even needed. Whenever you plan a meeting, make sure your purpose is clearly defined and invite only those who actually need to attend.

Follow this general format for planning a meeting:

- ✓ Decide the purpose of your meeting.
- ✓ Decide who needs to attend.
- ✓ Decide on the location based on the number of attendees.
- ✓ Prepare an agenda to keep everyone on track and email it to the attendees prior to the meeting.
- ✓ After checking with key participants, set the date and duration. Then notify all attendees of the details.

Lead Meetings Effectively and Efficiently

Unless you are waiting for a key person, always start on time, whether or not all members are present. Begin by welcoming the group and articulating the purpose. Establish ground rules by stating whether the meeting is open to discussion, if questions are allowed only after the presentation, if it is a brainstorming session, and so on. Stay focused on the agenda and do not get off track. Acknowledge each person's input, and allow time for all people to speak.

Make Good Use of Question and Answer Time

Asking good questions encourages participation, guides the direction of the discussion, enables you to keep control, and helps the group reach agreement. When planning your meeting, note questions you want to ask and check them off as the meeting progresses.

Maintain Control During Your Meetings

How much control you keep depends on the type of meeting you are conducting. Knowing how much control to maintain is one of the most important components of running a successful meeting. When planning the meeting, decide how you are going to control the discussion, move through the agenda, and reach agreement. Regain control when someone starts dominating the discussion by stating that you want to give everyone time to share their thoughts. Similarly, if someone is getting off track, tactfully interrupt and bring the discussion back to the agenda.

Understand Group Dynamics

In any group, norms will emerge. Norms are unwritten rules that dictate acceptable behaviors by the group members. People who deviate from the accepted norms will typically be dealt with through peer pressure. Someone who sits in the wrong chair might be expected to move. Someone who always arrives late to meetings might be given a project no one else wants to do. Norms also establish a pecking order within the group. Learn how the attendees will fall in the pecking order. This will enhance your understanding of the group. Watch who talks, who is quiet, and what nonverbal communication cues are given. Groups are most successful when the leader understands the dynamics of the group and encourages all members to actively participate.

Conclude Meetings by Energizing Attendees

When planning the meeting, plan the ending, as well. If possible, include a closing time in the agenda, and make sure you tell the attendees how much time will be allowed for discussion. When the ending time is approaching, start summarizing. Discuss accomplishments, review individual and group commitments, and confirm actions to be taken. Thank the group for attending. End by saying something positive, such as *You did a great job coming up with a solution that will work! Thank you.*

In Every Meeting, Talk Customer Service

No matter what the purpose of your meeting is, always relate your content to your customers.

Some ways to incorporate customer service into your meetings are:

✓ Discuss the impact of your agenda on customers.

✓ Ask a customer-related question to get everyone focused.

✓ Motivate attendees by recognizing outstanding performance.

✓ Clear up confusion when employees handle requests in different ways.

✓ Share customer comments (market research).

✓ Ask attendees how a particular aspect of customer service can be improved.

SPOTLIGHT ON MANAGEMENT

A Better Way to Train

Kimberly works for a casual-dining restaurant chain, managing the dining room wait staff. Last week she attended a half day "train-the-trainer" class for a new order input computer program that all her servers need to learn. She felt the material was easy to learn and had no problems understanding the new system, but she also realizes that not everyone will learn well from merely watching the training DVD.

When planning the training session for the wait staff, Kimberly chose to incorporate all three learning styles. Because she is training her entire team, she needed to allow ample time to work through the training effectively. As the program was implemented yesterday, she scheduled her employees to come in ninety minutes before the restaurant opened to receive their training.

She played the training DVD, followed up by reviewing the key points, and included a question-and answer-discussion in which she encouraged her employees to share their thoughts. Finally, she demonstrated inputting orders on the new terminal, and then asked each server to take a turn. To make it fun, she asked the other team members to call out orders. Everyone had a good laugh at some of the outlandish orders, but Kimberly paid close attention to make sure each employee fully understood the new system.

She also planned to spend her entire evening in the dining room, so she completed some of her administrative tasks before the evening shift began. There were a couple glitches, but over all, Kimberly felt good about the way the evening progressed. She gathered her team together for a few minutes after closing and asked for their input. She made some notes and closed this short meeting by saying, "You guys are awesome! Thank you for doing such a great job, especially for making tonight a terrific dining experience for our customers."

CHECKLIST

STEP 1: Understand Learning Styles

- ✓ Visual learners learn by seeing
- ✓ Auditory learners learn by listening
- ✓ Tactile learners learn by doing
- ✓ People learn best when material flows logically
- ✓ Incorporate all three learning styles when possible
- ✓ Eliminate distractions from training

STEP 2: Prepare for Training Sessions

- ✓ Determine whom you need to train and analyze what you need to convey
- ✓ Plan your delivery method
- ✓ Prepare yourself for training
- ✓ Establish time frames for training
- ✓ Choose the right location

STEP 3: Train Thoroughly

- ✓ Train on technical skills
- ✓ Train on company policy and procedures
- ✓ Train on customer relations

STEP 4: Follow Up after Training

- ✓ Spend time with attendees afterward
- ✓ Look for teaching and training opportunities
- ✓ Train employees to conduct market research
- ✓ Training is continual

STEP 5: Conduct Productive Meetings

- ✓ Plan purposeful meetings
- ✓ Lead meetings effectively and efficiently
- ✓ Make good use of question-and-answer time
- ✓ Maintain control during your meetings
- ✓ Understand group dynamics
- ✓ Conclude meetings by energizing attendees
- ✓ In every meeting, talk customer service

THE REAL WORLD

Practice Lesson

Susanne is an owner/manager of a woman's fitness center. She completed a corporate training class for a new computer system that will provide members with detailed information about personal weight loss and workout data. The new program goes into effect next week, and she needs to train her team, all of whom are part-time employees. She has a training DVD and workbooks for each employee to complete. Corporate estimates the training will take four hours.

Help Susanne plan her teaching method. Because these are part-time employees, she does not have a good grasp of their learning styles. Include all aspects of how to cover the material to ensure that all employees understand the new system.

_____

_____

_____

_____

To help Susanne prepare for the training session, write an introduction.

_____

_____

_____

_____

Next, explain the purpose of the training and write the learning objectives.

_____

_____

_____

_____

Schedule the training. Plan the best time and day, whether to train as a team or as individuals, how much time to allow, and where to train.

_____

_____

_____

_____

Finally, plan some follow-up activities to make sure everyone is using their new skills correctly.

_____

_____

_____

_____

PERSONAL PLANNER

Thoughts, ideas, and goals on training:

_____

_____

_____

_____

_____

_____

_____

_____

_____

_____

_____

_____

_____

_____

_____

_____

_____

_____

_____

_____

_____

_____

6

Team Building for Success

Developing a cohesive team sets you and your employees up for success. Cohesive team members communicate well, support each other, solve their own problems, make good decisions, and take responsibility for getting results. Cohesive teams do not develop by themselves, though. They stand behind a strong leader, who has devoted the time to develop a group of coworkers into a united team. Together, they commit to high standards and achieve their goals.

You may already have a group of employees who get along and achieve results. You may wonder why it is important to invest more of your valuable time in team building. Why rock the boat when things are sailing along smoothly? But, even though you may find smooth sailing now, what happens when you run into stormy seas? What happens if your boat capsizes? Unless you take the time to develop your employees' abilities to communicate, cooperate, show creativity, and work as a cohesive team, when you run into problems, emergencies, or other unforeseen events, they may swim in different directions, each trying to stay afloat, floundering and faltering until you jump in and rescue them.

When you work through team building phases, team members learn to talk through and solve problems, make good decisions, and assume full responsibility for outcomes, including providing exceptional service to all customers regardless of "stormy seas" or other internal challenges.

Cohesive Teams Challenge Themselves to Give Their Best to Customers and Company

You have heard the saying that two can do it better than one. That is true, as long as the two (or more) are working toward the same goals. When you develop your employees into a team, working together to achieve the same goals, they will stand united and strong.

So how do you get started? First, learn the characteristics of cohesive teams so that you can identify, develop, and model these behaviors. Cohesive teams have an effective leader who provides guidance; a clearly defined purpose; honest, open communication; mutual trust and respect; well-defined decision making and problem-solving procedures; and a strong focus on goals and areas needing improvement.

Promoting "team think" will help you and your employees move from "me" thinking to "we" thinking. Using terms such as *Our team* and *We* rather than *You* and *I* fosters team thinking. When you apply the characteristics of strong teams to your daily interactions with your employees and establish an environment in which everyone is expected to contribute to the success of the team, you can begin to move your employees through the phases of team building.

Forming a cohesive team involves working through a series of phases, beginning with communication. Communication requires the most time and effort since you are working to instill an atmosphere of open, honest give and take among your team members. As your employees increase their comfort level with each other and are communicating effectively, they move into the cooperation phase, where mutual trust and respect develop. The team members will identify with each other, their relationships strengthen, and they feel committed to the team. They will begin to take more responsibility for their performance. When you see that they are making decisions and suggesting ways to improve, they are moving into the creativity phase. During this phase, they will take more risks, set challenging team goals, and take full responsibility for the success of the team. When this happens, they are a cohesive unit, working together as a self-functioning team.

When you reach this stage, your team building job is not done, though. You need to continue the process by spending time with them, providing guidance and support, ensuring they continue working as a cohesive team, and guiding them when they backslide.

Finally, by being a team player, you strengthen your team and show that you are an effective leader. Staying involved, volunteering to pitch in and help, and leading through a hands-on approach shows everyone you are a positive role model for your team. When you follow the steps below, you will build a strong team, united in achieving team goals.

STEP 1: Understand the Characteristics of Strong Teams

STEP 2: Promote "Team Think"

STEP 3: Form a Cohesive Team

STEP 4: Continue the Process

STEP 5: Strengthen Your Team by Being a Team Player

SPOTLIGHT ON MANAGEMENT

The Wrong Way to Build a Team

Brian works for a mortgage firm, managing two offices located in the same city. When he took over the second office at the beginning of the year, he held a meeting to discuss joint goals and to give the employees from both offices the chance to meet each other. After the meeting, Brian noticed some grumbling going on between the employees of the two groups. He heard some of the employees in Office A complaining that they pull more of the weight than the employees in Office B. When he was in Office B he overheard the employees gripe about the "attitudes" the members of A group displayed toward them. One even referred to the A group as "a bunch of bullies who think they're better than us." Afterward, the employees had little interaction with one another, other than to handle overflow work.

Because of the random interaction between the offices, Brian was not too concerned about the situation until the morning he received a call that one of the employees in the B office was rushed to the hospital for an emergency appendectomy. He was told she would be out for at least five weeks. Another employee in that office was scheduled for vacation beginning next week and could not change his dates because his airline and cruise reservations have a no cancellation policy.

Brian held a meeting with the A office to explain the situation. He told them that someone would need to work in the B office for the next two weeks while the employee was on vacation. Rather than stepping up and volunteering, the employees refused and then began to complain about the other group.

"No way, I'm not going over there. They're a bunch of morons."

"We already have to handle what they can't, and we have to clean up the paperwork they screw up. Now one of us is supposed to work over there?"

Brian became frustrated. "Look, I need your help. The other office will be down two people, and the remaining three won't be able to handle the workload. If someone doesn't volunteer, I'm going to have to assign one of you. The bottom line is that the work needs to get done."

When the grumbling continued, Brian said, "JJ, you have the lowest seniority so you're going."

As they were walking out of the conference room, Brian heard JJ say to a couple other employees, "He can force me to go, but he can't force me to do all their work. I can guarantee you I'm not going to work my tail off like I do here. Let that group pull their own weight for a change."

What Went Wrong?

Brian had known about the grumbling between the offices but was not particularly concerned about it. Because he did not see the value in devoting time to building a cohesive team, this emergency situation blind-sided him. Then, when he had to order JJ to work in the B office, JJ displayed a poor the attitude about going. Consequently, customer service will suffer and results will decline because his employees are working against—rather than with—each other.

What Could Make This Right?

Holding a meeting at the beginning of the year to discuss goals was a step in the right direction, but it was only the first step. This scenario has a lot of "could haves." Brian could have held frequent meetings so the employees began to identify with each other. If he understood the dynamics of strong teams, he could have instilled these values in his employees. Brian could have demonstrated the expected behaviors and spoken in terms of "we" and "our team." He could have promoted an atmosphere of open communication and respect and, as soon as he heard grumbling, he could have discussed the situation with the team members and communicated his expectations about them working together and supporting each other. By investing the time to work through the phases of team formation, Brian could have developed his two groups of employees into one united team.

STEP 1: Understand the Characteristics of Strong Teams

Before you begin building your team, become familiar with the common characteristics of strong teams. As you learn about them, think how you can incorporate each into interactions with your employees. When you do this, you take the first step in team building.

Cohesive Teams Begin with Effective Leadership

Leadership is provided by an involved manager who understands the value of building a unified team. The manager knows employee strengths and weaknesses and works with employees, both individually and as a team, to develop positive work skills. Leadership is also shared within the team. Team members know each others' strengths and capitalize on them to ensure the team's success. They work in a positive environment where leadership is shared between manager and team.

Cohesive Teams Have a Strongly Defined Purpose

Team members feel a deep sense of purpose and commitment, and they support the company and team mission. They take responsibility for creating a mission that defines the goals of the team. They set challenging goals and work with their manager to ensure all goals are achieved. The manager stays involved with the team and frequently talks about their mission and purpose to keep them on track.

Cohesive Teams Communicate Effectively

Communication is handled by creating a team mentality. The manager promotes an atmosphere where everyone feels safe sharing their points of view without fear of embarrassment or retaliation. Team members talk openly and honestly, and positive words are expected to be used when speaking with each other. Methods for handling meetings are well defined and all team members are encouraged to participate. Ground rules are discussed and everyone is expected to abide by these rules. Employees are encouraged to get to know each other on a personal level to foster strong relationships. The manager spends time with the team, effectively communicating and listening, as well as observing team interactions.

Cohesive Teams Respect and Trust Each Other

Team members genuinely care about each other and know they can rely on one another. They develop strong relationships and may feel more like family than coworkers. They are invested in making the team the best it can be and willingly support and assist other team members. The manager models these behaviors by respecting and trusting members to do the right thing. Together, they work to achieve team goals.

Cohesive Teams Have Well-Defined Decision Making and Problem Solving Procedures

Team members feel empowered to make decisions and solve their own problems. They feel open about discussing conflict and have effective resolution procedures in place. They rely on their manager to be a mediator and resource. The manager communicates the limits of decision-making authority and provides hands-on guidance when the team faces conflict.

Cohesive Teams Focus on Goals and Areas Needing Improvement

The manager works with the team to set challenging, relevant goals and commitments. Team members share responsibility to achieve goals. Goals often surpass corporate expectations. All team members are accountable for performing well and peer pressure is applied to those who do not. The manager focuses on team achievements and areas needing improvements, although employees are recognized and praised for individual achievements.

STEP 2: Promote "Team Think"

Promote a spirit of "team think," where all members are encouraged to communicate in terms of the team, rather than focusing on themselves. What is "good for the team" overpowers thoughts of what is "good for me." Stay involved with your team, and demonstrate that although you are its leader, you are also a member of the team.

Establish a Team Identity

Start by speaking in terms of "we" rather than "me." Use the words "our team" when talking to your employees and coworkers. When you form the habit of speaking in terms of team, your employees will pick up on your cues. Incorporate words that encompass your entire team as often as possible. Compliment employees when you see them supporting each other. Try to emphasize team efforts, team achievements, and team areas needing improvement whenever you can.

Model the Characteristics of Effective Teams

Discuss your team mission frequently and keep your team members involved in planning. Further open communication by being a good listener, by using positive language, and by expecting the same from your employees. Encourage a respectful environment by being respectful. Build a climate of trust by showing your employees that you trust them. Teach your employees how to make good decisions and solve problems effectively, and share responsibility with them. Work with your team to achieve goals.

Create an Enthusiastic, Positive Work Environment

Foster a supportive culture where everyone works together and helps each other. Look for opportunities to help others. Be the leader others come to for help. Ask what you can do to help rather than looking for help from others. Expect your employees to help one another. When you observe positive behaviors, thank your employees for pitching in. Give credit to your employees for team accomplishments.

STEP 3: Form a Cohesive Team

Building a team that effectively works together to achieve common goals takes time. You are not only changing your mindset, behaviors, and the manner in which you operate, you are changing your employees as well. As the team leader, you are going to guide your employees to move through the phases of team development: communication, cooperation, creativity, and cohesiveness. You will not be able to set a time commitment to work through each phase, but you will be able to identify where they are in team development and you will know when they have achieved cohesiveness.

Instill Open, Honest Communication

The best way to further open communication is to spend time with your team. Use the word "team" when referring to them and emphasize that "team" means a collective unit in which each member has an equal voice. Hold frequent team meetings. Share what is going on and explain *why*. Talk about your team's mission, plan, and goals in every meeting. Discuss team achievements, progress, and areas needing improvement. Ask questions to encourage all members of your team to take part in meetings. Ask for their opinions. Assign agenda items to members so everyone has an opportunity to contribute. Make it a rule in every meeting that no idea, comment, or question will be laughed at or ridiculed.

When you need something done, ask rather than tell. While you are working toward building trust and respect, continue to monitor and act on the needs of individuals. Expect your team members to support each other and communicate in a positive manner. When conflict arises within the team, resolve it immediately and work with those involved to find a win-win solution. Expect members to be honest and open with each other, particularly when resolving conflict.

Get to know your employees on a personal level and encourage them to get to know each other. As their communication skills with each other increase and they get to know each other better, camaraderie will develop.

Remember that communication is two way. Listen closely and pay attention to nonverbal cues. Encourage and guide everyone to communicate and participate in discussions openly, positively, and honestly.

Open Communication Develops into Cooperation

When you see that your team trusts and respects each other, cooperation among members will increase. You will observe them helping and supporting each other, and they will begin to solve problems independently. Teach your team how to find effective solutions and guide members to work through conflict in a positive manner.

They will want to take on additional responsibility for team achievements. Delegate more, but first, clearly define your expectations and train them to handle the additional responsibilities. Be available to help and support them.

With added responsibility, your team will take more pride in its work. Members will become more committed to each other and to making your team the best it can be. Tell employees how much you appreciate their commitment in taking on more responsibility. Set your team up to succeed and, when they do, acknowledge their successes, show your appreciation, and praise team efforts.

Cooperation Fosters Creativity

As relationships strengthen, the team becomes more united and will take full responsibility for outcomes. When your team members take responsibility for themselves, they will want to have input in how to reach team goals. Allow their creativity to flow freely. Encourage an atmosphere of creative thinking, and teach them how to set relevant goals. Now it is time for you to let go and allow the team the independence to try things its own way. Understand that mistakes will be made and conflict may ensue, so be prepared to provide the guidance and support to get members back on track.

Delegate more decision making power to the team members. This is not to say you will shift all decisions to them; rather, define the limits of their decision-making authority. As long as they feel empowered to share in some decisions, they will feel valued and vital to the overall success of the company. If you do not agree with a decision, ask open-ended questions and guide them through the decision-making process. Encourage them to think of themselves as the owner of the company when they form conclusions. This will help them think about all aspects and impacts of their decisions.

Allow your team members to plan and lead meetings. During this phase, your leadership role may evolve into more of a resource for your team. Your role is to support them, praise achievements, monitor for weaknesses, ensure that everyone has an equal voice, and guide them to success. Remember that when you give your team members more control over their results you must give them more freedom to make decisions.

Communication, Cooperation, and Creativity Lead to Cohesion

You will know you have reached cohesion when goals are achieved, team members come to you less frequently for help, it is easier to delegate work, progress continues in your absence, people outside your team give you positive feedback, and morale and commitment are high. Your main role now is to be a strong leader and cheerleader. Lead when they get off track. Cheerlead when they succeed. Consider yourself to be the energy source that drives your team.

STEP 4: Continue the Process

When you reach the cohesion stage of team development, it can be easy to feel complacent. Your team relies on you less often to solve problems. The members work together to make their own decisions. They set team goals that surpass company goals. You understand that your role is evolving. When they succeed, you praise them, and when they get off track, you lead them back. Now that you have extra time, update your plan to include team observation and analysis in your schedule. The only sure way you can guarantee they maintain this level of performance is to actively stay involved as their leader, and if they fall back, you should be prepared to work through the phases again.

Spend Time with Your Team

The most effective way to know what is going on is to spend time with your team. Observe, talk, ask questions, listen. Observe how your team members interact with each other. Look for teaching opportunities. Talk to them about their performance. Ask for their ideas and input. Listen closely to their answers. Be open to their suggestions, and act on practical ones. Foster an environment of independent and creative thinking.

Stay Active in Problem Solving and Conflict Resolution

Respect everyone's right to differing opinions and expect the same from your team. Allow members to work through problem solving and conflict resolution but be available to help. Praise employees when they work through problems and conflicts effectively and, when they cannot, mediate the process. Staying active in resolution is an assurance that your team maintains cohesion.

Analyze What You Can Do to Maintain Cohesion

Continually monitor your mission and plan and update as necessary. Monitor team goals and, when your team achieves them, work with them to set new ones. Monitor your team's interaction both within and outside the team to make sure members continue to perform as a cohesive unit.

Work Through the Team Building Stages When Necessary

By staying actively involved and observing your team members' interactions, you will know if they start to backslide. This frequently occurs when new members join a team or when new procedures are implemented. Any change in the dynamic of a team can cause a breakdown in cohesiveness. When this happens, analyze what phase the team is at and work from that point forward to the cohesiveness phase. As you can see, team building is not a one-time project. To remain successful, you must remain a strong force as your team's leader.

STEP 5: Strengthen Your Team by Being a Team Player

Cohesiveness is the glue that binds your team together. As the team leader, you need to ensure the bond stays strong. Every member of the team, including you, must work together for the team to succeed. Take responsibility for your team's success by observing, supporting, encouraging, and guiding them.

Let Your Team Know They Can Depend on You

Be a hands-on manager, and spend quality time with your team. Show your loyalty by supporting and encouraging team members. Be your team's booster by keeping a smile on your face, maintaining a consistently high energy level, being sincere, staying actively involved, and fostering an environment of open communication, trust, and respect.

Never Be Above Doing Any Job

Ask how you can help, listen closely, and provide the assistance your team members need. Be a hands-on leader, who is readily available to help. Never expect your team members to do something you would not do. Roll up your sleeves, pitch in, and help out whenever you can. Be a "do as I do," not a "do as I say," leader.

Always Show Appreciation for a Job Well Done

Give credit where credit is due. Praise both team and individual achievements. Speak constructively when giving corrective feedback. Set the bar high when setting team goals and expectations, and assure your team members you know they can achieve them. Never allow yourself or your team members to become complacent.

Do Something Every Day to Show Your Team You Value Them

Celebrate with your team. Praise good performance. Encourage new employees as well as those showing improvement in their personal development. Find ways to show your high-performance employees you value them. Break the routine and find ways to have fun. Do things to make your employees feel good about coming to work every day.

SPOTLIGHT ON MANAGEMENT

A Better Way to Build a Team

Brian works for a mortgage firm, managing two offices located in the same city. When he took over the second office at the beginning of the year, he knew these two offices had not interacted well in the past, so he immediately updated his plan and goal sheet to include time for team building.

He held a meeting for the purpose of discussing joint goals, but more importantly, he began team building by creating a team identity. Throughout the meeting, he used the words "we" and "our team" and focused on what the employees had in common. Then he paired employees from each office to form partnerships. He outlined his expectations, which included that the partners talk to each other at least once a week to share what was going on in their respective offices. He ended by saying, "Even though you work in two offices, we are one team. We need to communicate with each other and most importantly, we need to support each other. I will spend time in each office and with each of you. Remember that the only way we are going to achieve our goals is to work together."

Brian kept his promise to divide his time between the offices, and he devoted time to spend with each employee. He fostered open communication between the offices by holding monthly meetings. One of the agenda items was to ask each pair of partners to share something they had talked about.

He was pleased when he observed the team members speaking respectfully, and he also noticed trust developing. He used the March meeting as a teaching opportunity to talk about solving problems. He cited specific examples where partners had resolved issues with little guidance. He encouraged all members to try solving their problems and resolving conflicts but stressed that he would always be available to assist.

At the April meeting, when the partners were sharing things that had occurred during the past month, one of the pairs challenged the others to a goal competition. They jokingly bantered but the team came up with its own rules and set the duration of the competition. Brian sat back and observed and allowed the team to control this portion of the meeting. He left that meeting with a huge smile on his face, knowing that his team was moving into the creativity phase by taking responsibility for achieving its goals.

This morning, when he received a call that one of the team members in the B office was rushed to the hospital for an emergency appendectomy and another employee was scheduled for vacation the next week, Brian held a meeting with the A group to explain the situation. Before he could ask for a volunteer, Robert said, "I live the closest to that office so I'll go."

Two other employees volunteered as well, but since Robert was the first to step up, Brian said, "Thanks everyone. Robert, since you live the closest it makes sense for you to go."

Brian knew that his team would pull together to achieve the same level of service, even being down two employees.

CHECKLIST

STEP 1: Understand the Characteristics of Strong Teams

    ✓ Cohesive teams begin with effective leadership

    ✓ Cohesive teams have a strongly defined purpose

    ✓ Cohesive teams communicate effectively

    ✓ Cohesive teams respect and trust each other

    ✓ Cohesive teams have well-defined decision making and problem solving procedures

    ✓ Cohesive teams focus on goals and areas needing improvement

STEP 2: Promote "Team Think"

    ✓ Establish a team identity

    ✓ Model the characteristics of effective teams

    ✓ Create an enthusiastic, positive work environment

STEP 3: Form a Cohesive Team

    ✓ Instill open, honest communication

    ✓ Open communication develops into cooperation

    ✓ Cooperation fosters creativity

    ✓ Communication, cooperation, and creativity lead to cohesion

STEP 4: Continue the Process

    ✓ Spend time with your team

    ✓ Stay active in problem solving and conflict resolution

    ✓ Analyze what you can do to maintain cohesion

    ✓ Work through the team building stages when necessary

STEP 5:   Strengthen Your Team by Being a Team Player

    ✓ Let your team know they can depend on you

    ✓ Never be above doing any job

    ✓ Always show appreciation for a job well done

    ✓ Do something every day to show your team you value them

THE REAL WORLD

Practice Lesson

Megan manages a team of ten service representatives who handle billing inquiries for an electric utility company. She has worked hard to build her group of employees into a cohesive team. Yesterday her boss told her that another manager will be on loan to a different department indefinitely and, during this time, Megan will take over responsibility for three of that manager's employees. Megan was disturbed by the news because this manager has not done anything to develop her employees into a united team; therefore, Megan is concerned that bringing these employees, all of whom have negative attitudes, into her workgroup is going to cause her team to backslide.

Today, when she held a team meeting to share the news and ask for their cooperation, she was not too surprised by the responses. "You've got to be kidding. Of all the employees, we had to get the three worst?" "I'll tell you right now, I cannot work with Janet. She has the worst attitude and just the other day she told me off." "The same thing happened to me. She yelled at me about the way I handled a customer." "And have you heard how she talks to customers? I can't believe her manager lets her get away with that." "Well, what about Paul? He's no better." The team continued to complain as they left the meeting. Megan knows she has her work cut out for her.

Help Megan build her new team back to the cohesive stage. Begin at the communication stage. What are some things Megan can do to foster open communication?

_____

_____

_____

_____

Megan is observing that the team members are now communicating openly and are speaking respectfully to one another. How can she further the cooperation she is beginning to see?

_____

_____

_____

_____

Now that the team is cooperating with each other, what can Megan do to encourage creativity?

_____

_____

_____

_____

When Megan sees her new team working cohesively, what should she do to maintain the unity?

_____

_____

_____

_____

PERSONAL PLANNER

Thoughts, ideas, and goals on team building:

_____

_____

_____

_____

_____

_____

_____

_____

_____

_____

_____

_____

_____

_____

_____

_____

_____

_____

_____

_____

_____

7

Dealing with Challenges Successfully

Whenever people work together, challenges will occur, and a smart manager is always prepared to deal with them. It may be a disagreement among your employees, a misunderstanding between you and another manager, an employee who is exhibiting poor behaviors, dealing with change in the workplace, or being caught off guard by an unforeseen event. If you are prepared for challenges, you will be able to clear up misunderstandings, resolve disagreements, turn around poor performance, work through change, and deal well with emergencies and crises. Mastering effective resolution skills will ensure that your team continues to give your customers exceptional service.

Being Prepared for Any Challenge Keeps You on Top of Your Game

Whatever the cause, handling challenges effectively can be good for everyone involved. Overcoming challenges brings an opportunity to grow and develop. Effective resolution can strengthen relationships, increase productivity, enthuse people, promote the flow of new ideas, and increase understanding and knowledge.

When you recognize a challenge, take ownership of it, and work to find the best solution, you demonstrate that you are a leader who is unafraid of conflict. In your management role, you will find occasions when you need to step in and help others work through conflict by mediating an issue to resolution. When you take the time to listen to all sides, you will be able to frame the problem. Then you can decide and plan how best to resolve the conflict. When you meet with the involved people, you will be in a position to help them reach consensus, resulting in a win-win resolution.

When the conflict involves you, you are likely to be emotional or feel passionate about your point of view. As a result, reaching agreement and finding a win-win solution becomes more difficult. For example, a coworker may have taken credit for a project you completed, your boss may have assigned a project to you when you are already overloaded, or your employee may have spoken rudely to you during a meeting. Whenever a conflict situation involves you, communicating your feelings while keeping your emotions under control will open a dialogue and enable you to listen to what the other person has to say. Looking at the situation from the other person's perspective helps you find a workable resolution.

No matter how effectively you train, how well you motivate, and how often you provide feedback, you will, at some time, deal with an employee who does not perform up to par. When you determine the root cause for the poor performance, you will be able to work with the employee on an improvement plan. Taking time to think how to discuss the matter with the employee, what questions to ask, what questions need to be answered, and getting the employee to take ownership of the situation enables you to agree on the best resolution.

Change is inevitable and means stepping out of your comfort zone. That is never easy. Learning how to move through any change process is important in your leadership role. As the leader of your team, you are responsible to help yourself and your team members work through the stages of change, while remaining objective, consistent, and accountable for outcomes.

An anticipated challenge can be handled effectively through careful and thoughtful planning, but what happens when the unexpected is thrown at you? Anticipating things that might happen will help, as will developing contingency plans for emergency situations. It is most important, as a manager, that you remain calm and in control at all times. Doing so enables you to employ your critical thinking skills when quick decisions are called for.

When you arm yourself with effective resolution skills, you will be prepared to handle any challenge, including these:

STEP 1: Mediate Conflict Involving Others

STEP 2: Resolve Conflict Involving You

STEP 3: Turn Problem Performers into Peak Producers

STEP 4: Handle the Change Process

STEP 5: Expect the Unexpected

SPOTLIGHT ON MANAGEMENT

The Wrong Way to Handle Challenges

David manages a team of eight service employees who handle medical billing records for various physicians' offices. Last week his boss met with all the managers to share the news that their small company has been bought out by a firm headquartered in another state. The merger will take place in three months. In the meantime, it is business as usual until they receive training on new billing procedures. "Look," said David's boss, "this is a big company, and it is a good move for us. I need you to share the news with your employees right away before the grapevine runs rampant. Put a positive spin on it, and assure everyone that this change will be good for us."

David left the meeting, still processing the news. He was supposed to stay positive for his employees, but he was not feeling very positive. *What if the new owners decide it's too expensive to keep our office open? What if we lose our jobs? I've got a wife and two kids, what if I can't pay my bills?* David tried to quell the unease he felt in the pit of his stomach as he ran through his list of what-ifs.

Although he was still dealing with his own emotions, when he got back to his office he gathered his employees together. He smiled as he spoke and stayed upbeat. "I just got great news that our company has been bought by Apex Billing Services headquartered in California, effective March first. This is a large company, and it's going to be really terrific for us."

He was met with blank stares. Slowly, his employees began to digest the information.

"California? That's across the country. You know they're not going to keep our small office open."

"Do you think we'll lose our jobs?"

"Whoa! Look, there is no need to worry. I've been assured that we're staying put. We need to learn the new company's computer program to be on board with its billing practices. Period. This is going to be a great change for all of us!" David felt good that he was able to put such a positive spin on such unsettling news.

Later that day, David heard one of his employees sharing some news about Apex. He had heard that Apex had bought out another company the size of theirs and within one year that office was closed. David researched the rumor and assured his team that it was false, but that did not seem to help. Everyone continued to mope around, convinced they would lose their jobs. Again, David reassured his team.

One week passed and David's team and the company's other three teams were still moping around. Productivity had declined. The consensus of the entire office was that they would be out of jobs. David got upset with his team and this morning blasted them. "I told you that rumor was not true. Only one department in that office closed and all the employees were given other jobs. If you don't get off this kick and start working, we *will* be out of jobs. Now I need all of you to stop talking about this and get to work."

What Went Wrong?

Sugarcoating news of a change, particularly such shocking news as a company buy-out, is never the correct approach. It is natural for people to feel uncertain, confused, and scared. David thought he did the right thing by keeping the talk light, and staying positive and upbeat even when he felt uncertain, confused, and scared. He underestimated how everyone was going to feel and, when they displayed the same emotions he had, David did nothing to help his employees begin working through the change process.

What Could Make This Right?

Any change, whether it is welcome or unforeseen, means moving out of your comfort zone. Changing means giving something up and you always need time to mourn your loss before you can embrace the new. David's manager could have handled this better by saying to the management team, "While I believe this will be a good move for us, and we've been assured that no jobs will be cut, we need to be sensitive to our employees' emotions. This is a huge change, and they are likely to feel shocked and scared. When you talk to them, give them the facts that we know and allow them time to process the news. Be sensitive to their feelings, and take the time to listen and speak with them about their concerns. I want you to stay positive when you talk to your employees, but don't try to sugarcoat the news. That approach isn't going to work. Likewise, don't get caught in the negativity trap. I've printed out some material on working through the change process. Let's read through it so that we understand the phases of change. That way, you will be able to help yourselves and your employees accept this change and move forward." Then, the management team could determine the best approach to share the news and begin working through the change process.

STEP 1: Mediate Conflict Involving Others

If you are uncomfortable facing conflict, welcome to the club. Most people feel uncomfortable when dealing with any conflict, but especially when it occurs in the workplace. In your position, you are likely to be the one to mediate conflict situations that involve your team. It might be a situation involving two of your employees who do not get along, an employee who feels another employee is not doing his or her fair share of the work, or a group of employees who are upset with one of their coworkers for whatever reason. Managers often ignore these situations, hoping the problem will go away. The bad news is that ignoring conflict only allows it to grow and eventually become unmanageable. If left unresolved, conflict causes those involved to become disgruntled and bitter, it causes relationships to break down competely and, in the worse-case scenario, you can lose your customers. When you effectively resolve problems, you gain respect as an involved leader committed to being part of the solution rather than part of the problem.

Anticipate Problems and Deal with Them Immediately

Conflict often arises as a result of poor communication, misunderstandings, or disagreements between people. Someone may feel slighted, left out of the loop, or unfairly treated. In high-producing teams, conflict may arise when people are creative, productive, and feel passionate about their work. Be on the lookout for conflict, and work to resolve the situation immediately, when the problem is still manageable. Become an active observer, stay involved, and watch for things that do not seem right. Ask your team members and coworkers to tell you when a problem is brewing. Be aware of employees or coworkers who suddenly become negative, quiet, agitated, or upset, as this can be a sign of conflict.

Frame the Problem

Before attempting to draw conclusions or make decisions about a situation, gain a complete understanding of the problem. Allow those involved, individually, to tell their version of the story. Listen carefully to all sides. Ask questions to gain understanding.

Pay attention to the nonverbal messages you are receiving—as well as those you are sending. People are going to be emotional when talking about a conflict, so observe the message behind the words. Is the person angry, hurt, embarrassed? What is the person actually telling you? Keep your own emotions in check and remain objective. See the situation from all sides. Understand where each person is coming from. When you have heard all sides, you should be able to frame the problem.

Decide and Plan How to Resolve the Conflict

When you are confident you have enough details to work toward resolution, take time to think through the situation before deciding how to respond. It may help to "rest" the problem for a short time so you can make the best decision. When you have drawn your conclusion, plan what you will say when you meet to mediate and guide the discussion. Think how those involved are going to respond, both to each other and to you. Who will be confrontational? Who will be passive and quiet? Plan how to maintain control of your mediation meeting.

Next, decide who needs to attend the meeting and where it will be held. If the conflict is between two people, you most likely do not need to involve your entire team to resolve the issue. When choosing where to meet, find a private location that is free from distractions.

Find a Win-Win Solution

The most effective way to resolve conflict is to allow those involved to jointly reach consensus. Facilitate the discussion and encourage everyone to present their sides and listen to each other. Ask questions to draw out the responses, and guide them to reach consensus. Work toward a solution that everyone can buy into. When complete agreement is not possible, make sure everyone accepts the final outcome before adjourning the meeting.

There will be times when consensus cannot be reached. If tempers flare or those involved cannot reach agreement, give everyone time to calm down by adjourning and meeting later. If, after meeting again, it is still impossible to reach consensus, you may have to make the final call in order to move forward. In that event, stress that you listened to all views and take the time to explain the reasoning behind your solution to the problem. Gain consensus that each person understands and accepts your decision. Even though some may not agree with it, helping them understand where you are coming from and why you came to that conclusion should help everyone buy into it.

STEP 2: Resolve Conflict Involving You

If the issue does not involve you directly, it should be easy to stay composed. What happens, though, when you are involved in the conflict and have trouble controlling your emotions? When this happens, maintaining self-control and objectivity can be an unrealistic expectation, yet it is crucial to resolving the problem.

Keep Your Emotions in Check

Your reflex reaction may be to respond immediately, yet it is important to maintain self-control and not respond until you have had time to think through the situation. Learning not to be reactive will help slow your racing heart and racing thoughts. Make it a rule to always take time to think through a situation. If you have to, walk away rather than lose control of your emotions. This will keep you from lashing out in anger or saying something you will later regret. When you have calmed down, think about how you want to resolve the issue.

Communicate Your Feelings

Consider how you want to communicate your point of view. Speak in terms of how the issue made you feel and how it affected you. Do not assume you are right and the other person is wrong. Only state the facts as you know them and discuss how you view the issue without assigning blame. *During my presentation at yesterday's meeting, you said that one of my ideas was stupid. I felt belittled and embarrassed. That comment really threw me off for the rest of my presentation and, today, I can't stop thinking about it. I'm still upset by your behavior.*

Listen to the Other Side

Listen carefully to what the other person has to say. Really listen. Pay attention to nonverbal messages. See the situation from the other person's vantage point and, if need be, put yourself in the other person's shoes. Often, when we do this, we can view the situation completely differently. Your coworker responds: *You gave a solution that I knew couldn't work. I had tried something similar with my team, and it backfired. In retrospect, I shouldn't have said it was a stupid idea, but because experience had taught me it wasn't going to fly, I just blurted that out.*

Work Together to Find a Workable Solution

You listened to the other side. You paid attention to nonverbal messages. You looked at the situation from the other person's perspective. Now, find a workable solution that you and those involved can buy into. Be clear when making your recommendation. *I understand and appreciate that you had a different point of view. Next time, though, I'd be grateful if you would allow me to finish my presentation before saying something. I'd also appreciate if you could phrase your comments more objectively.* Make sure everyone is in agreement before resting the issue. Your coworker takes responsibility: *Look, I'm really sorry for saying that. I'll make sure not to interrupt in the future and to keep my comments more constructive.* Say something so that everyone can move forward on a positive note: *I'm just glad we resolved this so we can move on.*

STEP 3: Turn Problem Performers into Peak Producers

Dealing with a problem performer can be unnerving. If a problem continues after you have provided sufficient training, followed up, spent time with the employee, and provided constructive feedback, you have a problem performer on your hands. In all likelihood, the problem performer does not see a need to change, so it is up to you to get the employee to take ownership for changing his or her behavior. Unless you take necessary steps to turn around poor performance, the situation is not going to correct itself, your other employees will see you as being weak, and they may lose respect for you. To correct poor performance or a poor attitude, deal with the situation head on.

Determine the Root Cause for the Poor Performance

Before confronting the employee, think about the exhibited behavior. You want to take time to diffuse your reactive anger and uncover the reason for the poor performance. Generally, poor performance can be linked to a lack or misunderstanding of training or a lack of motivation to perform well. Analyze the facts to make a root cause determination. Focus on the situation you observed and specifically on the behavior exhibited. Has the employee been properly trained? Does the employee possess the necessary skills to adequately perform the task?

Plan Your Meeting

When you identify the reason behind the problem, you will be able to plan what you will say when you meet with the employee. If you conclude the employee has not received the proper training, you can explain what you observed and schedule the training.

If, however, you identified the reason as a lack of motivation to perform well, you have a problem performer to deal with. When you meet, you will want the employee to explain the reason for the behavior and take responsibility for changing it. It can be helpful to write out a framework for your meeting, including some open-ended questions. Try to picture how the employee may respond. What is the worst case scenario? Predicting an employee's reaction will help you stay calm and in control during the meeting. Will the employee become defensive, angry, sullen, or subdued? Play out each situation in your mind to avoid any surprises. Picture yourself calmly responding to various reactions, always remaining focused on the exhibited behavior.

Describe the Behavior

When you meet with the employee describe the behavior you observed. Stay focused on the behavior, not the person or personality characteristics. Just state the facts as you know them and speak in an objective, unbiased manner. *Bob, yesterday I observed you speaking in a condescending tone to a customer. Then, today, another customer you spoke with called back very upset because she felt you were rude to her. I was able to calm her down but this should not have happened.*

Ask the Employee to Explain

Next, ask the employee to explain the reason for his or her actions. This gets the employee talking and will help you to understand the reason for the employee's behavior. Be direct and to the point. You have no reason to beat around the bush or sound apologetic when questioning poor performance. *Why did this happen yesterday and again today?*

Listen to the Response

Listen and let the employee do the talking. This may be difficult because you are used to taking charge of situations. It is crucial, though, to let the employee explain the reason for his or her behavior. Resist the urge to put words in the employee's mouth. If the employee is silent and does not answer immediately, stay silent as well. Wait for the response. If the employee responds by saying something like, *I'm sorry; I realize I've been short with people. I'm having a rough time at home but I will make sure this doesn't happen again,* you can move on to the next step. The employee has taken ownership for the problem and has given you the correct resolution.

If the employee does not take ownership or merely says, *I don't know,* ask open-ended questions to keep the employee talking. *Why do you think both the customer and I felt you used a rude tone?* The employee's response will determine how you will proceed. *I get frustrated when customers ask me about our return policy because I'm not clear on what to tell them.* In this scenario, you have uncovered a training opportunity. *I get tired of customers who want everything done yesterday.* You now know the employee needs an attitude adjustment.

Agree on the Resolution and Give a Positive Affirmation

Before you can agree on a resolution, the employee must take ownership for correcting the problem. Continue to ask questions until you see that he or she understands that the performance is unacceptable. *What will happen if we do not value each customer?* Again, allow the employee the time to answer. Guide him or her to do most of the talking. When you see that the employee understands the need to change the behavior, ask *what will you do differently in the future?*

Now you can agree on what the desired behavior should be. If you have concluded that the employee needs additional training, schedule the training session. If you have concluded that the employee needs a change of attitude, state clearly how you expect customers to be treated. Review the correct procedures and cite any pertinent written guidelines. If necessary, update the employee's development action plan. Finally, affirm to the employee you have confidence that the performance will improve.

STEP 4: Handle the Change Process

In life, one thing is certain: change is inevitable. It may happen expectedly with hope and anticipation or it may happen unexpectedly with shock and fear. At work, change can blindside any organization. It can quickly deteriorate customer service, productivity, and morale. It may only take an instant for change to occur, but it takes time to adjust to it. You must work though a series of stages before you can move into a new comfort zone. The better prepared you are to deal with change, the better prepared you will be to move through and lead your employees through the process with courage and confidence.

Process the News

No matter how much you might like things to remain status quo, they are not going to stay that way. The truth is there is little you can do about change. Any change, even a change that you welcome, is going to force you out of your comfort zone. As a result, you may feel a sense of loss and declining confidence. Whether you are implementing the change or life throws you a curve, the quicker you can process the news and move into a problem-solving mode, the quicker you will regain your confidence and move forward.

People process change in various ways. Some thrive on it, some adapt easily, some struggle to accept it, and some do not handle it well at all. While thriving on change may not be your style, learning to be adaptable and flexible will enable you to process it more easily. Take time to adjust to what is happening, and go easy on yourself as you work through your emotions.

Accept the News and Move Forward

Once you have processed the news, you can regroup and move from feeling confused and uncertain to being ready to deal with the change head-on. Ask yourself crucial questions, such as: *What needs to be done? What do I need to learn? What resources can I depend on? Who needs to be involved? How much time do I/we have? How can I help others?* Asking these questions will help you keep your emotions under control and think more objectively so that you can move into a problem-solving mode.

Understand the Stages of Change

Recognizing what you are feeling and dealing with your emotions will enable you to take responsibility for helping yourself and others involved in the change. Learn the stages of the change process to recognize the emotions you and your employees may be feeling, and identify what stage you and your employees are in. The common stages of change are denial, sadness, resistance, exploration, and acceptance.

- In denial, people have trouble accepting the change. This emotion may range from wishful thinking—*The other company may not buy ours out*—to complete refusal to accept the facts—*There is no way this is going to take place.*

- As reality sets in, it is natural to feel sad. *Our company will never be the same. We'll lose the family atmosphere.* Feelings may range from slight sadness to an overwhelming sense of despair.

- When people are sad, they resist the inevitable. A sense of turmoil may emerge. "Me-centered" emotions surface. *What's going to happen to me?*

- Resistance eases into a more objective viewpoint. *My manager said our office isn't closing. It wouldn't make much sense with the customer base we have.*

- Objective thinking leads to exploration. *Working for a larger company could be a good thing. Being part of a large corporation may bring new opportunities.*

- The last stage of the change process is acceptance. *I'll make the best of this, no matter what happens.*

When you identify what stages your employees are in, you will be in a position to help them move into acceptance. Listen well, and show empathy and concern. Encourage everyone to talk. Help your employees look at the change objectively. Include them in problem solving and planning meetings. When you see that they are accepting the change, help them look ahead to the end result and set goals for the future.

Remain Objective

Your role as a leader is to understand the stages of the change process and help others who are struggling, but let's face it. You are human and need to deal with your own emotions. Thoughts of *what's going to happen to me* may surface. When this happens, talk to someone who can help you. A huge benefit of talking through any situation is that it helps you view things from different perspectives.

Look at the change from all angles: the customers, the organization, the employees. Ask: *what can I do to make things better for everyone?* If your job is to present the change to your employees or customers, speak objectively. Present both the positive and negative sides. Listen to the feedback and respond truthfully. Avoid phony sincerity, such as selling the change—*This is going to be great!*

Maintain an upbeat attitude to help workplace morale. Give your employees and customers extra care during the transition. Stay close, pay attention, listen carefully, and stay supportive of other people's emotions.

Stay Accountable for Outcomes

In times of turmoil and confusion, it is easy to let things slide. Deadlines may pass. Customer service may decline. Your energy level may wane. You may become easily distracted. During times of change, stay focused on your work, your employees, and your customers. Analyze your responsibilities and keep yourself on target until things return to normal. Focus on your personal needs by making sure you get enough rest, exercise, and eat well. Look beyond yourself to the big picture. Look ahead to the end result and envision your workplace when the change is behind you.

Prioritize your work so that you can devote time to functions that are important. Spend more time with your employees. Talk to them and listen actively. Ask for their suggestions, ideas, and input. Cut out nonessentials during periods of change and focus only on the necessary.

STEP 5: Expect the Unexpected

It is difficult enough dealing with challenges, such as conflict or change, when you have time to plan, but what happens when you get hit with the unexpected? What happens when something blindsides you or the change is so disturbing that the challenge seems insurmountable? You might get news that one of your employees was involved in a tragic accident on the way to work and died, a fire damaged your office and destroyed records, or half of your workforce called in sick with the flu. At times like these, learning how to prepare for the unexpected will help you move forward as a confident, strong leader.

Anticipate Problems

Things may be sailing along smoothly, but as a manager, you know that rough seas may be just around the next bend. Something, sometime, somehow is going to happen that will toss you and your team into stormy seas. Staying involved, asking questions, and looking for things that are amiss will help you anticipate problems that may be developing. The sooner you can deal with any situation, the easier it is to work through it.

Employ Critical Thinking Skills

Critical thinking is reflective thought about issues and situations that may have no clear-cut answers or solutions. When you employ your critical thinking skills, you will consider problems carefully before making decisions; ask questions to clarify the issue; analyze all arguments or proposed solutions; verify the credibility of the source; make value judgments about all possible solutions; keep an open mind and stay objective; decide on the best action; and communicate your decision effectively. On face value, these steps appear to take a lot of your time, but the more you employ your critical thinking skills, the less time it will take to arrive at good solutions.

Develop Contingency Plans

This is probably the most important step for handling emergency or crisis situations. You may think of a crisis as a large-scale circumstance that affects many people; however, most crises actually occur on a much smaller scale. A crisis may be something as small as how to handle the workload when an employee calls in sick. Learning to think proactively keeps you from thinking reactively. Think about worst-case scenarios and how you would handle them. Put in place contingency plans for unforeseen events that could occur and make sure everyone involved understands their roles.

Remain Calm and in Control

During a crisis or emergency, your number one rule should always be to remain calm. You will not do anyone any good if you lose your temper or become unglued. Take a deep breath—or a few. Figure out how much time you have to think out your plan of action. Put your critical thinking skills to good use. When time permits, ask others for their ideas and help.

When time does not permit, make the decision for your team but first, think of the worst-case scenario for the action you are going to take. Help others remain calm by staying calm and in control.

A Better Way to Handle Challenges

David manages a team of eight service employees who handle medical billing records for various physicians' offices. Last week his boss met with all the managers to share the news that their small company has been bought out by a firm headquartered in another state. The merger will take place in three months. In the meantime it is business as usual until they receive training on the new company's billing procedures.

David's manager then said, "While I believe this will be a good move for us, and we've been assured that no jobs will be cut, we need to be sensitive to our employees' emotions. This is a huge change, and while I want you to stay positive when you talk to your employees, don't try to make light of the news. On the other hand, don't get caught in the negativity trap. I've printed out some material on working through change. Let's read through it so that we understand the stages of coping with change. That way, we can help ourselves, and you will be able to help your employees move forward."

As a team, they reviewed the stages of the change process and agreed that each manager would hold a meeting the following morning so that all employees would receive the news at the same time. "Be prepared for people to feel shocked and scared when you break the news. When you talk to them, tell them the facts that we know and allow them time to process the news. Take the time to listen and talk to them about their concerns."

David left the meeting, still processing the news, but because he now understood the stages of dealing with change, he knew that his feelings were normal. David tried to quell the unease he felt in the pit of his stomach as he ran through a list of what-ifs. Later that day, he talked the situation over with another manager, a step that helped him think more objectively.

The following morning he met with his team to tell the members about the merger. He spoke in a confident, assured manner. "I just received news that our company has been bought by Apex Billing Services headquartered in California, effective March first. This is a large company, and we have been assured that our office will stay open. We will need to learn Apex's billing program and procedures, but that is the only change we need to deal with."

He was met with blank stares. Slowly, his employees began to digest the information. David continued, "I understand this is a huge change we're going through. Frankly, when I heard the news, my immediate reaction was to feel shocked and scared. Now that I've had time to digest the news, I realize that once we get on board with the new procedures, nothing else is going to change for us. We will continue to operate our office as we always have."

"Do you really think they'll keep our office open?"

"Yes. We've been assured that our office will stay open. There is no reason they would close us down. Apex has bought out other small firms, and they have all stayed open. There is no reason to believe it won't be the same for us. Right now, let's focus on doing our best, learning the new system, and becoming a vital part of Apex."

David closed the meeting by stating that if anyone wanted to discuss the merger one on one, his door was open. Whenever someone came to him with concerns, he listened and talked objectively, which helped his employees calm down.

David made time in his daily planner to spend extra time with his team. When it came time for the training to begin, he was confident that his employees had moved into the exploration or acceptance stage of the change process.

CHECKLIST

STEP 1: Mediate Conflict Involving Others

✓ Anticipate problems and deal with them immediately

✓ Frame the problem

✓ Decide and plan how to resolve the conflict

✓ Find a win-win solution

STEP 2: Resolve Conflict Involving You

✓ Keep your emotions in check

✓ Communicate your feelings

✓ Listen to the other side

✓ Work together to find a workable solution

STEP 3: Turn Problem Performers into Peak Producers

✓ Determine the root cause for the poor performance

✓ Plan your meeting

✓ Describe the behavior

✓ Ask the employee to explain

✓ Listen to the response

✓ Agree on the resolution and give a positive affirmation

STEP 4: Handle the Change Process

✓ Process the news

✓ Accept the news and move forward

✓ Understand the stages of change

✓ Stay accountable for outcomes

STEP 5: Expect the Unexpected
      ✓ Anticipate problems
      ✓ Employ critical thinking skills
      ✓ Develop contingency plans
      ✓ Remain calm and in control

THE REAL WORLD

Practice Lesson

Jessica manages six employees at a women's clothing store. A week ago, one of her employees told Jessica that another employee, Randi, ignores customers when they come into the store. Jessica was surprised because she had trained Randi and the last time she observed her, things seemed fine. Jessica assured the employee that she would handle the situation. This morning she observed Randi turn her back on a customer who came into the store. She busied herself folding sweaters and continued to ignore the customer. Jessica intervened, greeted the customer, and helped her. After the customer made her purchase, Jessica felt angry with Randi, since she had made it clear during training that her job was to greet customers when they come into the store and then ask if she could help them find something.

Jessica needs to turn around the poor performance. After thinking about the behavior, Jessica feels that the root cause is a lack of motivation to perform well. Help her plan her meeting by writing down her opening statement describing the behavior and her question asking Randi to explain.

_____

_____

_____

_____

Let's assume that Randi does not respond, but rather looks down. Jessica notices that she has an angry facial expression. What question should Jessica ask next?

_____

_____

_____

_____

Finally, Randi takes ownership by saying, "I know I'm supposed to do that but last week when I asked a woman how I could help, she said something rude to me. I figure if customers want something they'll ask." Write down an acceptable solution they might agree on.

_____

_____

_____

_____

What additional steps should Jessica take to ensure the poor performance is turned around?

_____

_____

_____

_____

PERSONAL PLANNER

Thoughts, ideas, and goals on dealing with challenges:

_____

_____

_____

_____

_____

_____

_____

_____

_____

_____

_____

_____

_____

_____

_____

_____

_____

_____

_____

_____

_____

PART THREE

MANAGING FOR RESULTS

8

Monitoring Performance for Excellence

Effective leaders get results. They hold themselves accountable for meeting customer, organization, and team goals. They understand how to get results through their employees' efforts, and they know that the most effective way to determine how well their team is doing is to monitor performance and measure results through involved management, direct observation, and analysis.

Your number one job is to make sure that your employees get the results you need. When you commit the necessary time to monitor team, employee, and personal results, you will stay on track to achieve your goals. Since your customers are the ones who are responsible for keeping you and your team employed, your number one goal should always focus on customer satisfaction.

Monitoring Performance Ensures Excellence for Your Customers

When your customers are satisfied, they are an asset to your company because people talk. Depending on the service they receive, your customers can be your best—or worst—marketing and advertising tools, so it makes good sense to provide exceptional service at all times. When you consistently measure results and monitor performance, you will be assured that everyone on your team is giving exceptional service to your customers. And that is your best guarantee that they say good things about your company.

First, you need to identify the results you need to measure and how you will measure them; reviewing your goal sheet can be an important tool. Some results can be measured quantitatively through reports derived from concrete figures, such as sales, revenue protection, accuracy, productivity, and expenses. Other results are measured qualitatively through direct observation, such as customer satisfaction, adherence to policies and procedures, interpersonal relations, oral or written communication, and accountability.

The only way you can effectively monitor performance and measure results and objectives is to stay involved with your team members and observe them directly. Unless you are a vital part of your team's day-to-day operation, you will have difficulty knowing specifically what is going on. Results may slip and your employees may lose their momentum. Scheduling observation time in your planner is crucial to hands-on management and monitoring your team's performance.

Directly observing your employees will enable you to determine the level of service they are providing to your customers, along with other subjective measurements that you include in performance appraisals. Your purpose in observing is twofold: you want to correct poor behaviors, as well as give praise and positive feedback for outstanding performance.

When you spend time with your employees, document any behaviors or actions that will have an impact on an employee's performance record and personal development. Documenting provides a reference point for individual feedback and performance appraisals. In addition, good documentation helps you spot individual and team trends and helps you correct problems.

Measuring objective results and observing your employees' contacts are the only ways you will know who is performing well and who needs to improve. Follow the steps below and you will monitor performance for excellence.

STEP 1: Measure Results and Objectives

STEP 2: Manage Hands-on

STEP 3: Observe Your Employees

STEP 4: Document Performance

SPOTLIGHT ON MANAGEMENT

The Wrong Way to Monitor Performance

Nicole works for a corporate event planning company. She is responsible for assigning individual projects to her four event planners, who then coordinate events from start to finish. The success of events is also Nicole's direct responsibility. Therefore, it is critical that she stays involved with her employees on all projects.

However, Nicole's boss asked her to personally coordinate a corporate training event for an important client. She willingly accepted the project, but soon fell behind in her other responsibilities. Finding time to monitor her employees was out of the question. Two weeks before the event, Nicole explained the situation to her employees. "For the next two weeks, I'm going to be even busier than I have been. I'll be finalizing all the details for this event. If anyone really needs help, or if something comes up that can't wait a couple weeks, I will try my best to make time to help you. But please . . . only something that absolutely cannot wait."

She was pleased that her employees understood and left her alone during this busy time. The day she was flying to the event she managed to spend a short time with them. She stopped by each employee's cubicle to check on the progress of projects. When she got to Melanie, who had only worked for the company for two months, Nicole noticed that she looked nervous and flustered and questioned her about it.

Melanie sheepishly replied, "I knew you were busy and I didn't want to bother you, but I'm way over my head with the Anderson Company project."

Nicole's mouth dropped open. The Anderson Company project was to plan a golf tournament weekend getaway for Anderson's top-producing employees. It was scheduled in one month. "Melanie, what exactly do you mean you're way over your head?"

"I'm having a problem getting the size banquet room Anderson needs because of another event the hotel is hosting the same weekend. The person I'm dealing with hasn't been a big help and now she's not returning my calls. I've left four messages. Because I haven't been able to finalize the plans, I can't get any of the promotional materials printed. The Anderson rep is getting upset with me. He doesn't understand what I'm going through."

"Have you escalated this to the hotel rep's manager?"

"No. I'm still waiting for the person to call me back. I didn't know what else to do."

"OK, look. I've got to leave for the airport in about fifteen minutes. Write down all the important details, and include the person's name and the number for me to call. I'll have to work on this tomorrow so we can get it resolved." Nicole was extremely flustered when she left. Tomorrow she should be able to devote all of her time to her own event but now she is going to have to work on Melanie's project.

What Went Wrong?

Nicole became so involved doing her own project that she did not spend time with her employees. Because she explained the situation to them, she assumed they were handling their workloads. Not taking the time to monitor their progress proved to be a costly mistake. Now Nicole has to worry about getting Melanie's project back on track when she should be concentrating solely on her own event. She is already feeling anxious about the event she is coordinating, so additional stress is something she does not need.

What Could Make This Right?

When Nicole's boss approached her to personally handle an important project, she could have communicated her needs with regards to taking on a project and finding time to monitor her employees. Asking her boss for assistance in scheduling her time so that she could keep up with all her responsibilities would have helped him understand how busy she would be. She could have asked for help either working on some functions of the project or with monitoring the progress of her employees' projects. Regular observation and follow up is necessary in her business, and she should not have assumed that her employees' projects were progressing on schedule.

STEP 1: Measure Results and Objectives

The only way you will know that you are staying on track to achieve your goals is to measure your results. Measuring results brings focus to achieving company goals, shows how effective you are, helps in setting new goals and monitoring trends, identifies input for problem analysis, gives employees a sense of accomplishment, and helps you monitor progress.

Determine What You Need to Measure

You only have so many work hours in a day, so focus on measurements in the order of their importance. Think about the overall picture: who, what, where, when, and how do you need to monitor and measure? Analyze your goal sheet to determine the answers to these questions. For example, if you manage a sales team, it is a no brainer that you are going to measure team and individual sales results. Similarly, in a billing environment, revenue protection is a critical measurement.

Most goal measurements will be obvious, but pay attention to the less obvious ones. For example, measuring sales can be accomplished through quantifiable sales figures, but you will also want to observe your employees to determine how well they are handling the sales portion of customer contacts. For each goal, think of all the ways you can measure and monitor for excellence.

Measure Both Quantitatively and Qualitatively

Certain measurements, such as sales and revenue protection, are derived from reports and can be measured quantitatively. To gain the best overall picture of how well your team is performing, however, you want to measure both results you can quantify and those that are qualitative, or based on your opinion. Let's say you manage an escalation team and measure individual results for handling times that can be quantified. In addition, you can observe your employees to measure how well they are performing through qualitative measurements. For example, during your observations, you can measure how well your employees determine the cause of the problem, find the best solution, and satisfy the customer. Subjective measurements from observations can help spot problem areas and turn around poor erformance.

Quantitative Measurements Are Based on Actual Documentation

Quantitative, or objective, measurements are results from data that you derive from reports. They include:

- Sales figures
- Revenue protection
- Accuracy
- Productivity
- Expenses
- Attendance

Measurements are concrete facts, figures, statistics, and percentages that cannot be disputed. They are useful for feedback and writing performance appraisals.

Qualitative Measurements Are Based on Opinion

Qualitative, or subjective, measurements are derived from observation and opinion, although they are often as important as quantitative measurements. They include:

- Adherence to established policies and procedures
- Interpersonal relations and the ability to work well with others
- Setting a positive example
- Oral and written communication
- Leadership abilities
- Personal career development tracking

Qualitative measurements derived from observation can actually be quantified for performance appraisals. First, create an observation form that includes all actions you will observe: how well the employee answers the call, handles the request (list the nuts-and-bolts items that your employees need to cover), and ends the call to make sure the customer is satisfied. For example, let's say that you noted five specific categories on your observation form. Assign a point value of twenty to each category. When you observe, score each item as you call it. Afterward, you will be able to quantify the measurement. Although it is still qualitative in nature —that is, it is based on your opinion—your opinion counts.

For other qualitative measures, you may elect not to assign a point system because measurements, such as setting a positive example and working well with others, may not be part of an employee's performance appraisal. Often, these types of observations are valuable considerations for promotions and other work assignments.

Measure Customer Service Results from the Customer's Perspective

Incorporating both objective and subjective measurements ensures that you are giving your customers exactly what they want. For instance, you may measure performance objectively through a call answer time monitoring system or by employing a company to conduct surveys that give you quantitative results. Whether or not your company uses external measurements, you will be responsible for measuring subjectively through direct observation and monitoring your employees for customer satisfaction.

Another valuable customer measurement tool is to train your employees to conduct market research (see Chapter 5, Step 4). When your employees listen to what customers are saying, relate the feedback to you, and you take action on important issues, you will continue to provide your customers with exceptional service.

STEP 2: Manage Hands-on

Unless you make time for your employees and monitor their performance, you cannot know if they are consistently providing exceptional customer service. Consistency is important. Spending quality time with your team one week but ignoring them the next is not hands-on management. When you commit to managing hands-on, your goal is to consistently monitor your employees. The quantity of time is not as important as the quality of time, so when you are with your team, make the most of it.

Schedule Team Time Every Day

Even if you can only spare a small block of time, team time should be considered a high priority every day. Make your attitude, *I'll make time now,* rather than, *I'll get to it later.* Unless you block out time with your employees, you will not get to it. You will find other tasks that keep you from your team.

You learned that as a manager, you get results through your employees. Only you can lead them to success. Left alone, they will flounder and lose direction. Leading them to success means spending time observing, coaching, motivating, and communicating with them. Remember that quality of time is more important than quantity of time, so even if you can only schedule 15 minutes on some days, make those 15 minutes count.

Give Your Undivided Attention

Your purpose in observing is to know how each member contributes to the team's overall success, so give each employee your full attention. Ask how they are doing, and find out in what areas they need help. Listen carefully and give them the help they need. When you spend time with your team, you may want to catch up on their personal lives, because this is a great way to build camaraderie and a cohesive team.

Always keep in mind, that although knowing your employees helps build team spirit, your objective is to monitor and observe goal achievement. Keep personal conversations short so that you can pay attention to your most important goal: monitoring and motivating everyone to provide exceptional customer service.

Communicate Goal Achievement

Talk about customer service when you are with your team, and communicate customer service goals and successes. Tell them how they are doing, both collectively and individually. When you are talking about areas in which your team excels, praise them and thank them for doing a terrific job. Choose positive words that motivate your team members to strive to achieve higher goals

When you are talking about areas in which your team has fallen behind, speak constructively and assure them you know they can achieve the team goals. Share specific ways in which they can improve. Choose words that uplift your team members, and make them want to do better.

Display Correct Behaviors

Whenever you are with your employees, whether you are spending time with them in their workspace, conducting a meeting, or having lunch with them, display correct behaviors at all times. Never forget that you are their leader, so show them how to act through your actions. When you are going to spend time with your employees, use visualization and self-talk to fully get yourself into your leadership role and picture yourself modeling correct behaviors.

If an employee makes jokes at a coworker's or a customer's expense, do not laugh or go along with it. If you laugh, your employees will see this as an acceptable behavior. Your team members will respect you more when they see that you are above laughing at someone else's expense. If an employee complains about a customer or another employee, remain objective and refrain from agreeing, ridiculing, or adding fuel to the fire. Stay out of gossip conversations, and never water a grapevine.

STEP 3: Observe Your Employees

Managing hands-on by scheduling time every day to spend with your employees, giving them your undivided attention, communicating goal achievement, and modeling correct behaviors are ways in which you lead your employees to achieve results. The most important task you can do when spending time with your team, though, is to directly observe your employees doing their jobs.

Know What You Need to Observe

When you review the items on your goal sheet, determine your employees' roles in achieving each goal. Note what you can observe about your employees' job performance, as well as how you can observe it for each function that you noted. Observing provides you with subjective measurements, so you want to pay full attention to the employee you are observing. This will enable you to make a correct determination of how well the employee is handling the customer contact.

When providing training, explain how you will observe a particular item. *Now that you've been trained on the discovery portion of sales contacts, when I observe your contacts, I will pay attention to see that you are using this training correctly.* Now you have taken the guesswork out of your observations, and your employees will know what you are paying attention to.

Stop, Look, and Listen

When you have an opportunity to observe your employees, stop whatever conversation you might be having and pay full attention. If you are speaking with another employee, give that employee the "just-a-minute" sign and start noting the details of the contact you are observing. Stop. Look. Listen. Paying complete attention is the only fair way you can assess an employee's performance.

Correct Poor Behaviors Immediately

When you see a situation in which an employee is doing something incorrectly, step in and provide guidance as to how it should be handled. If you determine that the employee has no clue what to do, take over the contact and handle it to completion while he or she observes. Afterward, take the time to reinforce the correct behavior through on-the-job or more in-depth training. Follow up to watch the employee performing the task.

Catch Your Employees Doing It Right

Your job includes ensuring your employees are well-trained, so they can perform their best. After training is complete, managers often focus more on changing incorrect behaviors than on praising correct ones. Noting your employees doing something well is a great motivational tool. People appreciate knowing how they are performing, so always remember to praise employees when you catch them doing something that exceeds expectations. Especially remember to praise your top performers. It can be something as simple as a pat on the back, a thumbs up, or a heartfelt thanks for a job well done.

STEP 4: Document Performance

Why take the time to document? You already have a busy schedule and finding time to spend with your team is difficult enough. You think you will remember all the details . . . and then you get bogged down, time passes, and you forget. Writing down the details immediately is necessary to correctly and completely document employee performance. When you provide feedback, you can cite the specific details. And when it comes time to write performance appraisals, you will have valuable backup data.

Document the Who, What, Where, When, and How

Because documentation is an important tool that provides a reference point for individual feedback and performance appraisals, include the following key points: date, time (if applicable), employee name, and a description of your observation or customer feedback. When you speak with the employee, either to correct or commend, make a note of your conversation and the agreed-upon action, if any is necessary.

Document Anything Out of the Ordinary

When documenting observations that you quantified, come up with a concrete percentage for how well your employees are performing. In addition, document both exceptional and improper performance—anything out of the ordinary that you may cover during feedback sessions. Document only your direct observations and employee commendations;

never document hearsay from another manager or an employee. If a co-worker refers a problem to you, follow up by observing and making your own determination of the situation.

However, if a customer brings a problem to your attention that was the direct result of one of your employee's actions, you should document the customer's comments and act on them immediately. For example, a customer found out that your employee knowingly assigned an incorrect due date, causing a delay in an order. You will want to determine why this happened, so discuss it with the employee by following the procedures discussed in Chapter 7, Step 3, for handling problem performers. If a customer commends an employee, document the customer's experience so that you can praise the employee.

Documentation Helps Spot Trends

In addition to using documentation for individual feedback and performance appraisals, use it to spot trends and patterns both for team and individual achievements. If your observations turn up a repeated problem, you will be able to analyze the cause and correct it. If your team or an employee is not meeting a goal, documentation may help you determine the cause and work with team members to improve.

SPOTLIGHT ON MANAGEMENT

A Better Way to Monitor Performance

Nicole works for a corporate event planning company. She is responsible for assigning individual projects to her four event planners, who then coordinate events from start to finish. The success of events is also Nicole's direct responsibility. Therefore, it is critical that she stays involved with her employees on all projects.

However, Nicole's boss asked her to personally coordinate a corporate training event for an important client. She willingly accepted the project, but after returning to her office and analyzing her workload, as well as her employees' workloads, she realized that she would need help with scheduling the time to do everything. She made some notes and then set up a meeting with her boss.

"I appreciate your confidence in me, and I'm excited about coordinating this project. You know I will give it my all, and I promise I'll do a great job. After I left your office yesterday, I reviewed both my and my employees' workloads. I'm concerned this new project will prevent me from finding adequate time to complete all my other tasks, as well as monitor my employees' progress on their own projects. Will you take a look at my planner and help me organize and plan my schedule?"

She then opened her planner for the next month. When her boss saw all that she had going on, he raised his eyebrows. "Wow. When I assigned this project to you I didn't realize all that you and your team have going on. I definitely want you to handle this project, though. You're the only one I trust with this important client."

"And I want to handle it," she assured him.

Together, they reviewed her planner. Her boss reassigned another of her projects and offered to help her monitor her employee's progress during critical phases when she would be unavailable to spend time with her team. Because Nicole was proactive and met with her boss, she was able to show him how overloaded her schedule was. Asking for help rather than complaining showed him that she was a positive leader who wanted to do an exceptional job, and he was more than willing to help her.

CHECKLIST

STEP 1: Measure Results and Objectives

✓ Determine what you need to measure

✓ Measure both objectively and subjectively

✓ Objective measurements are quantitative

✓ Subjective measurements are qualitative

✓ Measure customer service results from the customer's perspective

STEP 2: Manage Hands-on

✓ Schedule team time every day

✓ Give your undivided attention

✓ Communicate goal achievement

✓ Display correct behaviors

STEP 3: Observe Your Employees

✓ Know what you need to observe

✓ Stop, look, and listen

✓ Correct poor behaviors immediately

✓ Catch your employees doing it right

STEP 4: Document Performance

✓ Document the who, what, where, when, and how

✓ Document anything out of the ordinary

✓ Documentation helps spot trends

THE REAL WORLD

Practice Lesson

Andy manages the outside maintenance crew for a country club. His team of ten men is responsible for golf course, pool, and tennis court maintenance. Andy spends a lot of time training new employees, after which he spends time individually with each employee. When he spots an employee doing something wrong, he immediately retrains him or her. Then, he follows up to make sure the employee is performing correctly.

Yesterday, Andy's manager stated that the owners felt it would be a good idea for all managers to begin writing yearly performance appraisals on employees. Andy has never written down anything about his employees, and he has no clue where to begin. After thinking about what items he should appraise, Andy wrote down his crew's responsibilities for the golf course, which include cutting the grass twice a week to specified heights, trimming the greens daily, moving the pin and tee box markers daily, maintaining the sprinkler system, seeding, and fertilizing every month.

Now that Andy has determined the items he can include in his employees' performance appraisals with regard to golf course maintenance, write down some of the subjective items that Andy will be able to monitor. Frequently, the employees interact with members and guests, so write down some ways Andy can measure customer satisfaction.

_____

_____

_____

_____

_____

_____

List some ways in which Andy can spend time with his team for the purpose of observation.

_____

_____

_____

_____

_____

_____

During a ride-along, Andy observed that his employee, Jay, mowed the grass on the green to the correct height, but when he adjusted the cutting blade to mow the fairway, he began mowing the grass too short. Andy immediately stopped Jay and talked to him about it. Jay admitted that he knew the correct adjustment, but that he was in a hurry and had not taken the time to double check. Together they made the correct adjustment, and Jay continued mowing. Document the observation and discussion.

_____

_____

_____

_____

_____

PERSONAL PLANNER

Thoughts, ideas, and goals on monitoring performance:

_____

_____

_____

_____

_____

_____

_____

_____

_____

_____

_____

_____

_____

_____

_____

_____

_____

_____

_____

_____

_____

_____

_____

_____

9

Motivating Through Meaningful Feedback

The purpose of monitoring and observing is to improve substandard performance and reinforce good performance. This is accomplished by motivating through meaningful feedback.

Some managers motivate by handing out awards for a job well done. Others motivate by giving monetary incentives. Yet others motivate by rewarding employees with time off or other nonmonetary prizes. Handing out awards, incentives, and rewards may motivate employees, but these types of motivation are usually short lived and employees become conditioned to expect something just for doing their jobs.

Effective managers know that the best and longest lasting form of motivation occurs when employees are made to feel good about the jobs they do and believe that their performance contributes to the overall success of their company. These managers understand that the power of their words can uplift and motivate, just as easily as they can demoralize and deflate.

Meaningful Feedback Encourages Employees to Do Their Best

When you observe your employees, you provide two kinds of helpful feedback: constructive and positive. Both types, when delivered in a meaningful manner, will encourage employees to perform well. When giving constructive feedback, selecting words that maintain an employee's self-esteem and giving an assurance that you value him or her can be a great motivator. When giving positive feedback, something as simple as saying a heartfelt thank you can be a great motivator for a job well done.

Giving feedback that is meaningful and effective takes practice. The more you become accustomed to giving feedback, the easier it will be for you to say the words that make your employees feel valued and know that they are important to the overall success of your team. Effective feedback is always focused, specific, timely, and non-threatening; it also maintains the employee's self-esteem.

Feedback need not be long and drawn out. Quick feedback can reap positive results. Telling an employee about his or her performance right after you observe a behavior or action is most effective. Saying specifically what you liked about the performance, or what you did not like, and giving an honest accounting of the behavior enhances the employee's understanding of the feedback.

A good time to review employee progress is during feedback sessions. When you observe a behavior that needs to be corrected, discuss it with the employee. If you agree that action needs to be taken, you may decide to jointly create a development action plan. Noting who is responsible for taking action, what action needs to be taken, when and where it will be completed, and how it will be completed takes any guesswork out of responsibilities.

The most important feedback comes during the performance appraisal. Typically, formal appraisals are written, discussed with employees, and documented annually. When you determine what items an employee will be appraised on, you can create an appraisal form that will keep you focused throughout the year. When meeting periodically to discuss goal achievement, the appraisal form will also be a helpful tool for both the employee and you.

Your management role includes many opportunities to give feedback to others, but what happens when you are the on the receiving end? Learning to accept feedback graciously will help you come across as confident and in control at all times. Listening carefully and asking clarifying questions will help you process the feedback. Taking the time to analyze the feedback before acting on it puts you in the position of deciding whether or not to accept it.

Master the steps below, and you will give employees the powerful and meaningful feedback that will motivate them to perform their best at all times.

STEP 1: Meaningful Feedback Is Focused, Specific, and Timely

STEP 2: Quick Feedback Gets Positive Results

STEP 3: Development Action Plans Improve Performance

STEP 4: Appraising Performance Is the Most Effective Feedback

STEP 5: Accept Feedback Graciously

SPOTLIGHT ON MANAGEMENT

The Wrong Way to Give Feedback

William is a manager in a catalog call center. One of his duties is to observe his eight sales reps when they take customer calls. William blocks out time on his daily planner two days a week to be with his employees, so he can observe the required ten calls per employee per month.

When conducting employee observations, William pays close attention to performance items, such as answering the phone properly, interacting well with the customer, providing customers with correct and complete information, finding the best solution to the request or problem, inputting the order correctly, and ending the call by asking if the customer needs anything else.

William does a good job of giving corrective feedback. He is specific and gives feedback immediately after listening to a call. Today, he asked an employee to place a customer on hold and gave corrective feedback before the contact was completed: "When you were finished asking questions, I noticed that you didn't try to up-sell on any items. When you get back on the line, ask the customer if she would like the cardigan that matches the top." William showed the employee the information about the coordinating cardigan on the computer screen. Then he added a short training tip: "For most items, you'll see a coordinating piece. I want you to make sure that you always offer them to your customers."

The employee nodded, then went back to the customer: "Mrs. Jennings, thank you for holding. I wanted to mention that we have a matching cardigan for the sleeveless sweater you ordered. You can find it on page 16 of your catalog, and the two items look really great together. . . . Terrific, I'll add that to your order. I think you'll like the look of the coordinating pieces. All right, I've input all your items. What credit card will you be using?"

William finished observing the call and left without giving any further feedback to the employee.

Later that day he heard the employee grumbling about the observation session. "He has no problem telling me what I do wrong. I'd just like to hear what I'm doing right once in a while. I mean, why bother trying if you never hear anything good?"

William had an "aha" moment as he realized that positive feedback is just as important, if not more so, than corrective feedback. He realized that when giving corrective feedback without also giving positive feedback he was not doing a great job of motivating his employees.

What Went Wrong?

The danger in only giving corrective feedback is that employees feel managers only notice when they do something wrong and do not acknowledge when they are doing something well. When employees only hear the negatives, they may lose motivation, become disgruntled, and even lose interest in doing a great job. They might develop the attitude, *why should I bother trying if my good work goes unnoticed?*

What Could Make This Right?

Managers often find it easier to pick up on what an employee does wrong because a main responsibility is to develop employees and look for ways to improve performance. But it is human nature to want to be appreciated, and employees want to know when they are performing well. William does not need to give feedback for every call that is handled correctly, but he should look for opportunities to praise. At the end of the call, he could have said, "That was great. I liked the way you mentioned that the cardigan looks really nice with the sleeveless sweater. I think that's why the customer bought it." Then he could have assured the employee by smiling and saying sincerely, "Keep on doing that, and I'm sure we'll see a boost in your sales results." Going forward, whenever William observes, he should look for performance that he can praise.

STEP 1: Meaningful Feedback Is Focused, Specific, and Timely

Telling your employees how they are performing means sharing your observations and evaluating their performance. That can be difficult if you are not accustomed to giving feedback. Learning the components of meaningful feedback will help you compliment good behaviors and provide concrete suggestions for improving areas of weakness.

Meaningful Feedback Is Focused

Focusing on one area at a time keeps your message from being diluted. When you try to cover too many issues at once, your message may not be received completely or as intended. By focusing feedback on the most critical items, you can prevent this from happening. Focusing on the behavior rather than on the person or personality keeps your message objective. State what you observed by beginning your feedback with, *I noticed* or *I observed,* rather than with, *You did. You* statements may put the other person on the defensive, while *I* statements pave the way for honest dialogue. *I noticed that your tone became condescending when the customer sounded confused* or *I liked the way you explained the features of the computer program to that customer. Your enthusiasm really came through.*

Meaningful Feedback Is Specific

When you give feedback, provide specific details. Saying, *you did a great job,* or *that was terrible,* is too vague to be constructive. What was good? What was terrible? After giving the details, state what impact the behavior may have had on the customer. *I observed your last call. When the customer asked about our return policy, you first said thirty days. Then, you changed it to anytime with a receipt. If I was the customer, I'd be confused. The correct answer is that an item can be returned anytime, but the customer must have the receipt.* Likewise, when giving positive feedback, remember to tell the employee exactly what was good. *I thought you did a terrific job explaining our return policy to that customer. Based on her response, she clearly understood what you were saying.* By giving specific details, the employee knows exactly what you did or did not like about the contact and the behaviors are more likely to be changed or reinforced.

As you learned in the previous chapter, give feedback only on behaviors and performance that you personally observe. When someone tells you about a negative situation involving your employee, make sure the feedback is warranted before talking to your employee. Giving feedback based on hearsay is never advisable unless you have previously observed the same behavior or you know that the person providing the information is completely reliable. Something may have been taken out of context or the person may only have heard part of a conversation, so it is usually best to observe the employee in action before giving feedback.

Meaningful Feedback Is Timely

When you observe a behavior that needs to be corrected or praised, give feedback right away while you can recall all the details. When you observe a behavior that is unacceptable, such as an employee mistreating a customer, do not wait until later; rather, immediately discuss the situation with the employee. If you observe an employee behave rudely to a customer, but wait until the next day to discuss it, how many more customers will the employee offend? By waiting, you may lose your opportunity to motivate the employee to change the behavior and, in the worst case scenario, you may lose customers. When giving feedback, avoid mentioning something that happened yesterday or the week before, such as: *On the contact I just observed, I heard you speak in a brusque tone to the customer. You know, now that I'm thinking about it, I heard you use the same tone when I observed your call last week.* Bringing up an observation from the past that you have not discussed may make your employee wonder, *If it was so bad, why didn't you say something about it at that time?*

Meaningful Feedback Is Nonthreatening and Protects Self-Esteem

In addition to being focused, specific, and timely, meaningful feedback should protect a person's self-esteem. When you give feedback, refrain from being judgmental and avoid saying things like, *you always* or *you never.* Rarely is anything always or never, and those words often make people defensive. In addition, do not stereotype the person or apply labels that may be offensive, such as saying: *You must be an idiot if you think speaking to a customer like that is acceptable.* Allow the employee to respond and end corrective feedback on a positive note. Say something such as: *I'm sure now that you're aware of it, it won't happen again.*

STEP 2: Quick Feedback Gets Positive Results

Whenever you observe your employees, focus on finding them "doing it right." When you look for the positives, you will find many opportunities to give quick praise. Your employees will appreciate that you noticed and will want to repeat their positive behaviors.

Give Feedback in Private

It is never appropriate to give corrective feedback in front of others. If possible, choose a quiet location. If not possible, talking to an employee at his or her workstation is fine, as long as you speak quietly and others cannot hear. If customers are present, take the employee into a private location.

When praising an employee, however, speaking within earshot of others can be a great motivator for an employee. Just first be sure that your employees are comfortable hearing praise in front of others.

Say It in as Few Words as Possible

When you give feedback, be concise. Giving quick feedback gets results, so usually there is no need to belabor or repeat your point. If you observed a serious problem that requires lengthy feedback, creation of a development action plan, or additional training, tell the employee what you observed and schedule time for follow-up action.

Watch Your Tone and Body Language

If you are angry or upset about a situation, such as an employee mistreating a customer, or an employee whose behavior has not improved after you provided corrective feedback, keep emotions out of your voice and facial expressions. Take time to calm down. Think about how you want to talk to the employee. Speak respectfully, focus on the observed behavior, and remain composed when giving the feedback.

Be Sincere

Your goal as a frontline manager is to help your employees be their best. Sincerity, or its absence, comes through whenever you give feedback, so speak and present yourself in an earnest manner. For those who need to improve a behavior, speak frankly to show that you care and are there to help them improve. For those who consistently do things right, thank them in a heartfelt manner and find ways to show your appreciation; that will increase their desire to continue to perform their best.

STEP 3: Development Action Plans Improve Performance

Giving feedback opens dialogues that clear the path to improving performance. But how do you ensure the situation is going to improve? If you give corrective feedback on a minor issue and further observations show that the employee took responsibility for improving performance, nothing more needs to be done. For those occasions where the employee continues to perform poorly, a development action plan can be helpful.

The Employee Must Take Ownership

When quick corrective feedback has not worked and the employee continues the same behaviors, follow the steps in Chapter 7, Step 3, for dealing with a problem performer (see pages 000-000). You need to know if the employee needs training or a change in attitude. Work through the steps until you uncover the reason for the problem and the employee takes responsibility for the behavior. Unless the employee sees the need for a development action plan, writing one will be meaningless and will waste your time, since you are the one who will monitor the plan. Only when the employee agrees that the behavior needs to be changed can you work together to set concrete and specific goals for improvement.

Make It a Joint Project

All goals included in the action plan must be jointly agreed on; otherwise, they will be your goals rather than your employee's. Before beginning the process, explain what you will be doing and why it is important. When you create the action plan, include the details for each area of improvement:

- Who is responsible for the action
- What action will be taken
- When the action will be improved or completed
- Where the action will be performed
- How the action will be completed

Celebrate Achievements

Monitor goal achievement frequently and praise employees who are improving. For those employees who have written a development action plan, review it with them and ask them to tell you how they feel they are doing. Ask in what areas they feel they need help. When your employees see that their development is important to you, it will be important to them as well. Whenever goals are reached, acknowledge and praise their accomplishments.

STEP 4: Appraising Performance Is the Most Effective Feedback

Employees want to know how they are performing and how they are contributing to the overall success of the team and company, so if you have not been giving periodic performance appraisals now is the time to start. Appraisals tell employees how well they have performed during a designated time period.

Create the Appraisal Form

If your company does not have a template for an appraisal form, create one of your own. A "fill-in-the-blank" type of form works well. Include both concrete measurements, such as sales figures derived from reports, as well as subjective measurements from your observations. Keep up with your documentation for goal achievement during the appraisal period. This will make writing the actual appraisal easy because most of the results will already be filled in.

Determine a number system that you can apply to each result, such as using numbers one to four to evaluate performance. For example, one means that the employee has not met objectives, two means satisfactory performance, three means more than satisfactory performance, and four equates to outstanding performance. Use the numbers for each goal item to average an overall appraisal score.

Determine the Appraisal Period

Formal appraisals should be done at least every year. Typically, the appraisal period is a calendar year, beginning in January. Once the appraisal period has been designated, schedule a meeting with your employees to communicate both company and team goals. Give them a copy of the appraisal form, and discuss each item with them. As you learned in Chapter 3, this is also a good time for each of your employees to create their own goal sheet, which can be amended throughout the year if additional developmental needs are uncovered.

Discuss Goal Achievement Throughout the Year

Results and goal achievement should be discussed frequently over the course of the year. You want to set your employees up to succeed, and the best way to do that is to talk to them about how they are progressing toward meeting their goals. Encourage your employees to take responsibility for achieving their goals by having them review themselves quarterly throughout the appraisal period.

STEP 5: Accept Feedback Graciously

Giving feedback to your employees is one thing, but what happens when you receive feedback from others? Do you accept it graciously, or do you become defensive when someone gives you negative feedback about your performance? Learn not to take negative feedback as a personal attack. By learning to accept feedback as constructive, you strengthen your skills in giving feedback.

Listen Without Interrupting

To grow and develop, you need to know how others perceive your actions and behaviors. When someone starts giving you negative feedback, your reaction may be to interrupt, explain, or disagree. Don't. No matter the manner in which the message is conveyed to you, listen attentively. Consider that the person speaking to you may not understand the components of giving meaningful and helpful feedback. Consequently, what is being said may even sound like a personal attack on your character. Nevertheless, allow the person to finish, and listen without interrupting.

Thank the Person and Clarify What You Heard

No matter how the feedback was delivered, no matter how you may be feeling, thank the person. Before proceeding, make sure you understand the feedback you are receiving. If you are unclear about what was said, ask questions to clarify, and then recap what you heard: *Are you saying that not only this morning, but on other occasions I've ignored you when you asked me questions?* Keep your emotions objective, and do not defend or rationalize your behavior or action. Say that you understand what the other person is saying, and apologize if you feel that will help: *I'm sorry. I wasn't aware that I did that. Thank you for sharing that with me. Let me think about what may have happened, and I'll get back to you.*

Analyze the Feedback

After thanking the person and clarifying what you heard, take time to analyze the feedback before responding. It is usually better to wait to respond. This gives you time to analyze the feedback, as well as to consider the person's motivation for talking to you about it.

Decide Whether to Accept the Feedback

If you found that the feedback was justified, meet with the person to acknowledge that you agree and then say what you will do differently going forward: *You know, after thinking about it, you're right. Lately I think I've gotten so wrapped up doing my own work, I haven't spent adequate time with you. I appreciate that you brought that to my attention and, going forward, I'll do my best to pay attention to your needs.* On the other hand, perhaps the person who gave you the feedback is a high-maintenance employee who looks for reasons to complain. If you found that the feedback was not justified, meet with the person, acknowledge the feedback, and say something that allows the person to save face: *I just wanted to get back to you about our conversation yesterday. I wasn't aware that you felt that way and, again, I apologize for any misunderstanding.*

Keep in mind that a person's perception is his or her truth, so whenever you are the recipient of feedback, be open to what you are hearing. View any feedback as useful information for your development and growth and use the feedback to create or amend your personal development plan.

SPOTLIGHT ON MANAGEMENT

A Better Way to Give Feedback

William is a manager in a catalog call center. One of his duties is to observe his eight sales reps when they take customer calls. William blocks out time on his daily planner two days a week to be with his employees, so he can observe the required ten calls per employee per month.

When conducting employee observations, William pays close attention to performance items, such as answering the phone properly, interacting well with the customer, providing the customer with correct and complete information, finding the best solution, inputting the order correctly, and ending the call by asking if the customer needs anything else.

William does a good job of giving corrective feedback. He is specific and gives feedback immediately after listening to a call. Today, he asked an employee to place a customer on hold and gave corrective feedback before the contact was completed. "When you were finished asking questions, I noticed that you didn't try to up-sell on any items. When you get back on the line, ask the customer if she would like the cardigan that matches the top." William showed the employee the information about the coordinating cardigan on the computer screen. Then he added a short training tip. "For most items, you'll see a coordinating piece. I want you to make sure that you always offer them to your customers."

The employee nodded, then went back to the customer. "Mrs. Jennings, thank you for holding. I wanted to mention that we have a matching cardigan for the sleeveless sweater you ordered. You can find it on page 16 of your catalog, and the two items look really great together. . . . Terrific, I'll add that to your order. I think you'll like the look of the coordinating pieces. All right, I've input all your items. What credit card will you be using?"

William finished observing the call and said, "I think you did a great job offering the customer the matching cardigan. You told her what page she could find it on and when you told her how nice it will look with the sleeveless sweater, you made the sale. You handled that very well."

Because William gave quick corrective feedback and was able to give quick praise, the employee knows exactly what went well and what did not. Now he knows what he needs to change and what he needs to keep doing. William completed his required observations for the month, computed the percentage for the observations, and noted the figure on the employee's appraisal worksheet.

CHECKLIST

STEP 1: Meaningful Feedback Is Focused, Specific, and Timely

- ✓ Meaningful feedback is focused
- ✓ Meaningful feedback is specific
- ✓ Meaningful feedback is timely
- ✓ Meaningful feedback is nonthreatening and protects self-esteem

STEP 2: Quick Feedback Gets Positive Results

- ✓ Give feedback in private
- ✓ Say it in as few words as possible
- ✓ Watch your tone and body language
- ✓ Be sincere

STEP 3: Development Action Plans Improve Performance

- ✓ The employee must take ownership
- ✓ Make it a joint project
- ✓ Celebrate achievements

STEP 4: Appraising Performance Is the Most Effective Feedback

- ✓ Create the appraisal form
- ✓ Determine the appraisal period
- ✓ Discuss goal achievement throughout the year

STEP 5: Accept Feedback Graciously

- ✓ Listen without interrupting
- ✓ Thank the person and clarify what you heard
- ✓ Analyze the feedback
- ✓ Decide whether to accept the feedback

THE REAL WORLD

Practice Lesson

Kelly is a newly promoted manager for an insurance company. Her employees handle both phone and face-to-face customer contacts. Kelly is responsible for observing her employees' customer interactions. Her boss explained to her how to give meaningful feedback, which was helpful. Today, when Kelly was on a phone call with a customer, she overheard one of her employees use a rude tone when a walk-in customer asked a question. The employee answered the customer, "If you read the policy, you'd know that you aren't covered for that." Then, the employee sighed loudly. Before Kelly could end her call and intervene, the customer thanked the employee and walked out.

This was the first occurrence in which Kelly has to give corrective feedback to an employee. This employee normally handles her customers well. Kelly is going to give quick corrective feedback. List the components that will make her feedback meaningful to the employee.

_____

_____

_____

Write the statement Kelly might use when giving the corrective feedback. Include a statement that protects the employee's self-esteem.

_____

_____

_____

If the employee takes ownership for being rude and offers to call the customer to apologize, what might Kelly say to end the feedback session?

_____

_____

_____

PERSONAL PLANNER

Thoughts, ideas, and goals on giving feedback:

_____

_____

_____

_____

_____

_____

_____

_____

_____

_____

_____

_____

_____

_____

_____

_____

_____

_____

_____

_____

_____

_____

_____

10

Putting Your Best FACE Forward

Putting your best face forward means being the best you can be in any situation. The first nine chapters of this book have been devoted to helping you do that. You learned how to be the best manager and leader you can be in order to guide your employees to be the best they can be. You should feel confident that you have the necessary skills to be an effective manager who can lead your employees to success.

Now, what about you? What about your personal success? Think about your dreams for your future. Think about where it is you want to go, what it is you want to do. Perhaps your personal dreams involve promotion within your company. Perhaps they involve going back to school for a higher degree. Whatever dreams you may have, this last chapter is all about you. It is devoted to teaching you how to put your best face forward at all times so that you may fulfill your personal dreams.

Putting Your Best FACE Forward Sets You Up for Success

Being a great manager and leader helps you achieve team and corporate success, but to achieve the personal success you desire, you have to put your best FACE forward by **F**ocusing, **A**chieving, **C**aring, and **E**xemplifying.

When you stay focused, you seek out innovative ways to keep your momentum going so that you do not become stuck in a routine, mired in the day-to-day humdrum that comes with any job. Stay proactive and focus on your personal goals by looking for opportunities to learn and improve your skills, questioning the status quo and finding ways to make things better, and planning carefully.

You can achieve your goals once you understand the need to take control of your destiny. The first step is committing to your personal desires and then turning those desires into goals. In addition, you should take personal responsibility for yourself, committing to doing your best every day and demonstrating to others that you want to help them succeed.

Caring about yourself and others is crucial to anyone's success. When you show that you genuinely care, you send out positive energy and put your best face forward. Your thoughts control your attitude, so think positive thoughts and then project that attitude outward. Stay in a positive frame of mind by developing an attitude of gratitude. That increases the probability that you will fulfill your goals and dreams.

Exemplifying the best you can be helps you gain confidence. You will feel good about yourself and, when you feel good, it shows. Find ways to showcase your achievements and stand out from the crowd by volunteering for projects and committees. Create daily affirmations to help you envision the person you are becoming.

Focusing, achieving, caring, and exemplifying help you put your best face forward at all times, no matter the circumstances, and that is how you will achieve personal success.

STEP 1: Focus on Keeping Your Momentum Going

STEP 2: Achieve Your Goals by Taking Control of Your Destiny

STEP 3: Care for Yourself and Others

STEP 4: Exemplify the Best You Can Be

SPOTLIGHT ON MANAGEMENT

The Wrong Way to Put Your Best Face Forward

Savannah is proud that she consistently ranks in the top one percent of managers in her company. She understands her management style and strives to be a consistently participative manager. She is a strong leader who is committed to helping her employees perform their best. At the beginning of every year, Savannah updates her team's mission statement, creates a plan, and sets goals for the year. She communicates well with her employees, coworkers, and manager. Savannah takes time to properly train her employees, continually works to keep her team cohesive, and handles conflict successfully. She schedules time for employee observation and motivates her employees by giving meaningful feedback. On the surface, she is the ideal manager.

Savannah prides herself on her accomplishments and works hard to keep her top ranking. But . . . she is so focused on managing and leading her team that she does little to showcase her skills and accomplishments. Whenever upper management visits her office, Savannah stays busy doing her job because she feels that is what she is being paid to do. She believes that her accomplishments and ranking speak for themselves. Savannah is confident that upper management will take notice of her managerial strengths.

This morning Savannah's manager announced that one of her coworkers, Paul, has been promoted to work directly for the vice president. Savannah sat, stunned, wondering how this could happen. Although Paul and Savannah are both ranked among the top managers, her results are consistently higher than Paul's. Later, she spoke with her manager about the promotion.

"I don't understand how Paul was selected over me. My results are always better than his. Don't get me wrong, Paul is a great guy and an asset to our management team. I just don't get it that they would select him over me when my results are better."

Her manager said, "Savannah, your results are terrific. But you have to understand, when it comes to promotions, it's not only about the results. Paul stepped up and took on projects that would showcase his skills to upper management. He was always the one who volunteered to be our office spokesperson when we needed to give presentations to upper management. And whenever they visited our office, Paul was right there talking to them about our office accomplishments. He also found ways to tell them about his team's accomplishments. In other words, when it came time for promotion, Paul was the manager who stood out in their minds."

What Went Wrong?

As her manager pointed out, promotions are about more than results. Often, the person who does the best job of showcasing his or her talents is selected. Because Savannah did a great job managing and leading, she assumed upper management would notice and choose her for promotion. The moral of this story is that when it comes to recognition, one should never assume that doing a great job is enough. We all need to "toot our own horns" now and then.

What Could Make This Right?

Promotions often go to the employees who find ways to stand out from the crowd. Paul was adept at doing this. He understood that getting good results was not going to be enough for him to get ahead. By volunteering for projects and presentations, he showcased his skills to upper management, and when a promotion opportunity arose he was the person who stood out in their minds. Savannah has a right to feel upset, but if she takes the advice of her manager and finds ways to showcase her skills and talents, she will take charge of her destiny and future with the company.

STEP 1: Focus on Keeping Your Momentum Going

It can be tough to stay focused, especially when you are sailing along, working efficiently and effectively. When your days become repetitive, the same level of focus is hard to maintain. You can easily get mired in the day-to-day routine, the routine can become mundane, and this leads to boredom. Find ways to stay focused, such as varying the activities in your plan and planning your activities wisely. When you do this, you will find ways to keep yourself, your employees, and your coworkers interested and excited about performing well.

Keep the Momentum Going

Look for opportunities to grow. When you are performing well, do not become complacent. Rather, look for ways to strengthen your skills. Set new goals, and find innovative ways to reach them. Self-analysis can help. Begin by asking yourself the following questions:

- What can I do to improve my communication style?
- What skills do I need to develop or strengthen in order to continue growing?
- What classes can I take to continue my self-development?
- What projects or assignments can I volunteer for?
- How can I add value to my team, my company, and my interactions with customers?
- What interpersonal skills do I need to work on?
- What can I do to help others succeed?
- What support do I need from others?

When you answer these questions (and others you come up with), include them in your personal development plan.

Learn Continually

When you look for learning opportunities and view every day as a chance to learn something, you will be open to new possibilities. Try setting a goal to learn one new thing every day. Learn from every encounter and consider that those opportunities may be disguised. Children and elderly people are often our best teachers. When you are forced into a new situation or a situation about which you are not pleased, find the good in it and view it as a chance to learn new skills. When you look at learning as an important part of your growth plan, you will continue to focus on improving and developing as a person.

Question the Status Quo

When things are going smoothly, you may feel entitled to enjoy the ride. There is nothing wrong with that, as everyone needs a free ride now and then. But do not enjoy the easy times so much that you become too comfortable. Always find ways to make things better, even if they are already pretty good. Look for things that need to be changed, including those within you. Pay attention to bad habits you may be forming and do something to change them.

Stay Proactive

Staying proactive is not that difficult when you develop contingency plans to deal with emergencies. Planning enables you to stay focused and handle crises when they arise. Think about typical emergency situations that may occur, and plan how you will handle them. Continually thinking about the "what ifs" will help you identify situations in which you do not have the luxury of time to think through a solution. That helps you stay focused on your goals.

STEP 2: Achieve Your Goals by Taking Control of Your Destiny

The best way to achieve your goals is to take personal responsibility for your life, give each day your best, and always do more than you are asked. You are responsible for your achievements. You are responsible for the choices you make. You manage your behavior and attitude. In other words, you are the manager—of you.

Commit Fully to Your Desires

What do you want to be when you grow up? It does not matter how old you are when you ask yourself this question. Many of us move through our lives not fully committed to working on the things we want to achieve. Think about your career and personal aspirations. Do you have a personal mission statement and goal sheet to achieve those aspirations? If not, they may well stay on the dream side of your mind rather than on the goal-oriented side. Take time to think about and decide what you want to do and what you need to do to get there. Then, you can write a personal mission statement and goal sheet to move you toward your destiny.

Take Control of Your Destiny

When you take personal responsibility for everything you do, you will achieve your goals. You will not make excuses or blame others when things go wrong. You will understand that most of the turns your life takes are well within your control. Of course, unforeseen events will occur, but most of the time you control your destiny. Take responsibility for your thoughts, words, actions, and personal growth. Commit to being the best you can be at all times.

Help Others Succeed

You are the cheerleader for your team and helping your employees will come back to you tenfold. Helping others succeed in achieving team goals is going to help you succeed as well. However, when you sincerely have the desire to help your employees (and coworkers) succeed personally, you send a powerful message that you truly care about their wellbeing, that you are a self-confident, self-assured person who does not feel threatened when others do well. That attitude sets you up for personal achievement. When you help employees and coworkers achieve their individual goals, they will be more inclined to help you succeed in reaching yours.

STEP 3: Care for Yourself and Others

When you truly care for yourself and others, it shows. People will know that you genuinely appreciate them and are concerned about their well-being. When you show that you care by sending positive messages, you do as much for yourself, if not more, than you do for others.

Develop an Attitude of Gratitude

Have you considered that the way in which you view the world is the way the world views you? Think about that. How you see yourself has a direct effect on how you see the world and how you present yourself. How you present yourself to others directly correlates to how others are going to respond. If you expect negativity, you will receive negativity. Likewise, when you expect experiences to be positive that is what you will get. What you send out is what you get back. When you train your mind to think thankful thoughts, you exclude negativity from creeping in. Be thankful for everyone and everything in your life. When you are thankful and grateful, you will stay focused on your goals and will appreciate each achievement along the way.

Watch What You Think

Your thoughts control your attitude, and your attitude controls how others perceive you, as well as how you perceive yourself. Your self-perception can even affect your destiny. You may have preset goals, but unless you think you can achieve them you won't. Choose thoughts that are positive and focus on where you want to go. Think thoughts that move you toward your goals and create a mindset of contentment and inner peace as you envision yourself already achieving your goals.

Send Out Positive Energy

Energy is contagious and people are drawn to those who send out positive energy. When you maintain a high-energy level and communicate in a positive way, you send positive energy out to others. Think before you speak, and make sure the words you choose are positive ones. Always take the high road and communicate in a way that makes others feel good. When you make others feel good, you will feel good. When you make others feel good, they are more inclined to send positive energy your way as well.

Make Fun Time a Daily Goal

When you look at life as an adventure, you will reflect outward that life is exciting and fun. Consider that you work more effectively and efficiently when you enjoy what you are doing. Whether you are with your employees, coworkers, customers, family, or friends, look for opportunities to have fun. When you are focused on having fun, working toward your goals becomes more enjoyable. Try to schedule fun time every day, whether it is to have lunch with your coworkers, ice cream with your kids, or a quick phone call to a friend or mentor.

STEP 4: Exemplify the Best You Can Be

When you make the effort to be the best you can be, good things happen. Your confidence grows, you present a great attitude, and you display strong leadership qualities. When you put your best face forward, you will feel good about yourself, about others, and about the work you do. When you feel good, it shows. People notice your confidence and commitment to excellence, appreciate your upbeat attitude, and respect your leadership. When you form the habit of exemplifying your best, you will find yourself wanting to be your best all of the time, and your chances for achieving your personal goals greatly increases.

Find Ways to Showcase Your Achievements

First and most importantly, no one likes a braggart, but you can showcase your achievements without sounding boastful or arrogant. And, unless you tell others about your achievements, your efforts may go unnoticed. A humble way to showcase your achievements is to talk about your accomplishments in a manner that will be helpful to other people's success. For example, you could say something like this to a coworker: *When I changed my method of observing my employees, my sales results jumped ten percent. I'll be happy to tell you about the changes I made because I think they can help you too.* When discussing a problem, always offer a solution that worked for you. During a staff meeting you could say: *I know we've discussed the problem with employees coming back from break late. Here's an approach I tried with my team that's working well.* When you take a supportive approach and show others that you are interested in helping them improve, you will stand out in other people's minds in a positive way and show that you care.

Keep the Spotlight on You

Another way to showcase your achievements is to stay in the spotlight. Volunteer for projects and committees where you will involve yourself with upper management or employees from other departments. When you attend meetings, always speak positively and stay solution oriented. Come to meetings prepared to speak about your role on the project or committee. Become a positive spokesperson for your team, department, company, and yourself. Whether or not your personal goal is to be promoted within your company, keeping the spotlight on yourself by being involving in interesting activities will increase your commitment to your company and your team, and you will find greater enjoyment in what you do.

Create Daily Affirmations

You learned in Chapter 2 that affirmations are statements of belief or declarations of truth. Affirmations can help you exemplify your best self. To put your best face forward at all times, write down your personal affirmations. Begin with the words *Today I am . . .* to create the picture in your mind that you are already putting your best face forward at all times. For example, *Today I am thinking before I speak so that I will be positive to everyone.* Envision yourself displaying these characteristics and qualities. Envision yourself sending out positive energy to your employees and co-workers when you speak to them. Include affirmations to help you stay focused, to help you achieve your goals, to show that you care, and to exemplify the person you want to be. Then you will exemplify your best face forward by giving your all in everything you do.

SPOTLIGHT ON MANAGEMENT

A Better Way to Put Your Best FACE Forward

Savannah is proud that she consistently ranks in the top one percent of managers in her company. She understands her management style and strives to be a consistently participative manager. She is a strong leader who is committed to helping her employees perform their best. At the beginning of every year, Savannah updates her team's mission statement, creates a plan, and sets goals for the year. She communicates well with her employees, coworkers, and manager. Savannah takes time to properly train her employees, continually works to keep her team cohesive, and handles conflict successfully. She schedules time for employee observation and she motivates her employees by giving meaningful feedback. On the surface, she is the ideal manager.

Savannah prides herself on her accomplishments and works hard to keep her top ranking. She also understands that she does not work in a vacuum and that being the ideal manager is not enough to get ahead in her competitive company. She has taken the time to think of ways in which she can showcase her strengths so that upper management will get to know her and recognize her contributions to the company.

Even though it is out of her comfort zone, Savannah volunteers for projects that will serve two purposes: strengthening her skills and allowing others to notice her accomplishments. She also volunteered to serve as the office spokesperson on a committee that meets with upper management on a quarterly basis.

This morning Savannah's manager announced that she has been promoted to work directly for the vice president. Because of her many accomplishments, no one was surprised by the news, and her coworkers were genuinely happy and felt that Savannah deserved the promotion.

CHECKLIST

STEP 1:   Focus on Keeping Your Momentum Going

- ✓ Keep the momentum going
- ✓ Learn continually
- ✓ Question the status quo
- ✓ Stay proactive

STEP 2:   Achieve Your Goals by Taking Control of Your Destiny

- ✓ Commit fully to your desires
- ✓ Take control of your destiny
- ✓ Help others succeed

STEP 3:   Care for Yourself and Others

- ✓ Develop an attitude of gratitude
- ✓ Watch what you think
- ✓ Send out positive energy
- ✓ Make fun time a daily goal

STEP 4:   Exemplify the Best You Can Be

- ✓ Find ways to showcase your achievements
- ✓ Keep the spotlight on you
- ✓ Create daily affirmations

THE REAL WORLD

Practice Lesson

This practice lesson is all about you. Write affirmations to help you put your best FACE forward at all times.

Write out some affirmations to stay focused.

_____

_____

_____

Write out some affirmations to achieve your goals.

_____

_____

_____

Write out some affirmations to show you care.

_____

_____

_____

Write out some affirmations to exemplify your best.

_____

_____

_____

Every morning, look in the mirror and repeat these affirmations. Envision yourself already confidently and comfortably doing these things.

PERSONAL PLANNER

Thoughts, ideas, and goals on putting your best FACE forward:

_____

_____

_____

_____

_____

_____

_____

_____

_____

_____

_____

_____

_____

_____

_____

_____

_____

_____

_____

_____

_____

_____

_____

INDEX